PROMOTING SECURITY IN WIRELESS TECHNOLOGY

HEARING

BEFORE THE

SUBCOMMITTEE ON COMMUNICATIONS AND TECHNOLOGY

OF THE

COMMITTEE ON ENERGY AND COMMERCE
HOUSE OF REPRESENTATIVES

ONE HUNDRED FIFTEENTH CONGRESS

FIRST SESSION

JUNE 13, 2017

Serial No. 115–38

Printed for the use of the Committee on Energy and Commerce

energycommerce.house.gov

U.S. GOVERNMENT PUBLISHING OFFICE

26–576 PDF   WASHINGTON : 2017

COMMITTEE ON ENERGY AND COMMERCE

GREG WALDEN, Oregon
Chairman

JOE BARTON, Texas
   Vice Chairman
FRED UPTON, Michigan
JOHN SHIMKUS, Illinois
TIM MURPHY, Pennsylvania
MICHAEL C. BURGESS, Texas
MARSHA BLACKBURN, Tennessee
STEVE SCALISE, Louisiana
ROBERT E. LATTA, Ohio
CATHY McMORRIS RODGERS, Washington
GREGG HARPER, Mississippi
LEONARD LANCE, New Jersey
BRETT GUTHRIE, Kentucky
PETE OLSON, Texas
DAVID B. McKINLEY, West Virginia
ADAM KINZINGER, Illinois
H. MORGAN GRIFFITH, Virginia
GUS M. BILIRAKIS, Florida
BILL JOHNSON, Ohio
BILLY LONG, Missouri
LARRY BUCSHON, Indiana
BILL FLORES, Texas SUSAN
W. BROOKS, Indiana
MARKWAYNE MULLIN, Oklahoma
RICHARD HUDSON, North Carolina
CHRIS COLLINS, New York
KEVIN CRAMER, North Dakota
TIM WALBERG, Michigan
MIMI WALTERS, California
RYAN A. COSTELLO, Pennsylvania
EARL L. "BUDDY" CARTER, Georgia

FRANK PALLONE, JR., New Jersey
   Ranking Member
BOBBY L. RUSH, Illinois
ANNA G. ESHOO, California
ELIOT L. ENGEL, New York
GENE GREEN, Texas
DIANA DeGETTE, Colorado
MICHAEL F. DOYLE, Pennsylvania
JANICE D. SCHAKOWSKY, Illinois
G.K. BUTTERFIELD, North Carolina
DORIS O. MATSUI, California
KATHY CASTOR, Florida
JOHN P. SARBANES, Maryland
JERRY McNERNEY, California
PETER WELCH, Vermont
BEN RAY LUJAN, New Mexico
PAUL TONKO, New York
YVETTE D. CLARKE, New York
DAVID LOEBSACK, Iowa KURT
SCHRADER, Oregon
JOSEPH P. KENNEDY, III, Massachusetts
TONY CARDENAS, California
RAUL RUIZ, California
SCOTT H. PETERS, California
DEBBIE DINGELL, Michigan

———————

SUBCOMMITTEE ON COMMUNICATIONS AND TECHNOLOGY

MARSHA BLACKBURN, Tennessee
Chairman

LEONARD LANCE, New Jersey
   Vice Chairman
JOHN SHIMKUS, Illinois
STEVE SCALISE, Louisiana
ROBERT E. LATTA, Ohio
BRETT GUTHRIE, Kentucky
PETE OLSON, Texas
ADAM KINZINGER, Illinois
GUS M. BILIRAKIS, Florida
BILL JOHNSON, Ohio
BILLY LONG, Missouri
BILL FLORES, Texas
SUSAN W. BROOKS, Tennessee
CHRIS COLLINS, New York
KEVIN CRAMER, North Dakota
MIMI WALTERS, California
RYAN A. COSTELLO, Pennsylvania
GREG WALDEN, Oregon *(ex officio)*

MICHAEL F. DOYLE, Pennsylvania
   Ranking Member
PETER WELCH, Vermont
YVETTE D. CLARKE, New York
DAVID LOEBSACK, Iowa
RAUL RUIZ, California
DEBBIE DINGELL, Michigan
BOBBY L. RUSH, Illinois
ANNA G. ESHOO, California
ELIOT L. ENGEL, New York
G.K. BUTTERFIELD, North Carolina
DORIS O. MATSUI, California
JERRY McNERNEY, California
FRANK PALLONE, JR., New Jersey *(ex officio)*

CONTENTS

PROMOTING SECURITY IN WIRELESS TECHNOLOGY

TUESDAY, JUNE 13, 2017

House of Representatives,
Subcommittee on Communications and Technology,
Committee on Energy and Commerce,
Washington, DC.

The subcommittee met, pursuant to call, at 10:00 a.m., in Room 2322, Rayburn House Office Building, Hon. Marsha Blackburn (chairman of the subcommittee) presiding.

Members present: Representatives Blackburn, Lance, Shimkus, Olson, Kinzinger, Bilirakis, Johnson, Flores, Brooks, Collins, Cramer, Walters, Costello, Doyle, Welch, Clarke, Loebsack, Ruiz, Dingell, Rush, Eshoo, Butterfield, Matsui, McNerney, and Pallone (ex officio).

Staff present: Kelly Collins, Staff Assistant; Blair Ellis, Press Secretary/Digital Coordinator; Chuck Flint, Policy Coordinator, Communications and Technology; Gene Fullano, Detailee, Communications and Technology; Jay Gulshen, Legislative Clerk, Health; Kelsey Guyselman, Counsel, Communications and Technology; Lauren McCarty, Counsel, Communications and Technology; Paul Nagle, Chief Counsel, Digital Commerce and Consumer Protection; John Ohly, Professional Staff, Oversight and Investigations; Dan Schneider, Press Secretary; Jeff Carroll, Minority Staff Director; Alex Debianchi, Minority Telecom Fellow; David Goldman, Minority Chief Counsel, Communications and Technology; Jerry Leverich, Minority Counsel; Lori Maarbjerg, Minority FCC Detailee; Jessica Martinez, Minority Outreach and Member Services Coordinator; and Dan Miller, Minority Policy Analyst.

OPENING STATEMENT OF HON. MARSHA BLACKBURN, A REPRESENTATIVE IN CONGRESS FROM THE STATE OF TENNESSEE

Mrs. Blackburn. Go ahead and call our subcommittee to order. And I will begin by thanking Mr. Doyle's Penguins for a very fine hockey series against my Nashville Preds. I told him I thought about bringing him a little bit of catfish today, but we were sorry we didn't win but we think it was just a fantastic series and we congratulate.

Mr. Doyle. Well, thank you.

Mrs. Blackburn. Yes. And now I recognize myself for 5 minutes for an opening statement. And I welcome each of you to the subcommittee's hearing titled, Promoting Security in Wireless Technology, and thank you to our witnesses for appearing and for offering your testimony on this important issue and thank you for submitting that testimony on time. We appreciate that.

Mobile connectivity has become essential to our daily lives as a result of technology and consumer demand. Unfortunately, increasing reliance on wireless devices and networks has provided more avenues for cybercriminals to compromise our security and harm consumers. According to the 2017 Hiscox Cyber Readiness Report, cybercrimes cost the global economy approximately 450 billion, and over 100 million Americans had their medical records stolen in 2016. I think that is such an important stat. 100 million Americans had their medical records stolen in 2016.

Threats to mobile devices and networks can run the gamut from the use of ransomware and phishing schemes to packet sniffing and attacks on encryption protocols used to protect information sent over WiFi. These incidents have been occurring with alarming frequency on scales large and small. The Harvard Business Review wrote last September 22nd that—and I am quoting—"Mobile devices are one of the weakest links in corporate security," and that "if mobile security isn't a problem for your company yet, it will be."

Hackers are smart. They are adapting. McAfee's 2016 Mobile Threat Report notes mobile devices are quickly becoming the cybercriminal's target of choice because of the abundance of sensitive information individuals store on them. This is corroborated by a Newsweek report from March that stated mobile ransomware attacks had already grown over 250 percent in 2017. The sophistication and frequency of cyber attacks against mobile devices continues to escalate and we must meet this challenge head-on.

Our hearing will also examine threats to wireless networks. As the Majority Memorandum notes, mobile devices generate numerous air interfaces to transmit data, with each interface creating unique security vulnerabilities and attack methods. Threats include packet sniffing, rogue access points, jamming, and locating flawed encryption algorithms. These attacks can be initiated by hackers to obtain financial information, user passwords, and block legitimate network traffic. A recent example of this was the DDOS attack against Dyn which disrupted websites such as Twitter, Netflix, and Etsy last November. We all remember that one.

I have often said that cyberspace is the battlefield of the 21st century. It is time to act. Hardworking taxpayers are demanding leadership from Washington in the cyber arena and it is our duty to provide it. Enhanced defensive capabilities should be developed by promoting greater collaboration between public and private entities.

CTIA has shown leadership through its Cybersecurity Working Group. Their efforts have brought Federal agencies such as the FCC and DHS together with the private sector to develop solutions to the dilemma. Whether it is encryption, the use of authentication standards, updating operating systems, or rigorous implementation of antivirus software, we must have an all-of-the-above approach when it comes to forging defensive strategies against cybercriminals.

[The prepared statement of Mrs. Blackburn follows:]

Prepared Statement of Hon. Marsha Blackburn

Welcome to the Communications and Technology Subcommittee's hearing titled "Promoting Security in Wireless Technology." Thank you to the witnesses for appearing to offer your testimony on this important issue. Mobile connectivity has become essential to our daily lives as a result of advances in technology and consumer demand. Unfortunately, increasing reliance on wireless devices and networks has provided more avenues for cyber criminals to compromise our security and harm consumers.

According to the 2017 Hiscox Cyber Readiness Report, cybercrimes cost the global economy approximately $450 billion and over 100 million Americans had their medical records stolen in 2016. Threats to mobile devices and networks can run the gamut from the use of ransomware and phishing schemes to packet sniffing and attacks on encryption protocols used to protect information sent over wi-fi. These incidents have been occurring with alarming frequency on scales large and small. The Harvard Business Review wrote last September 22nd that "mobile devices are one of the weakest links in corporate security" and that "if mobile security isn't a problem for your company yet, it will be".

Hackers are smart and they are adapting. McAffee's 2016 Mobile Threat Report notes mobile devices are quickly becoming the cybercriminals target of choice because of the abundance of sensitive information individuals store on them. This is corroborated by a Newsweek report from March that stated mobile ransomware attacks have already grown over 250 percent in 2017. The sophistication and frequency of cyberattacks against mobile devices continues to escalate and we must meet this challenge head on.

Our hearing will also examine threats to wireless networks. As the Majority Memorandum notes, mobile devices generate numerous air interfaces to transmit data, with each interface creating unique security vulnerabilities and attack methods. Threats include packet sniffing, rogue access points, jamming, and locating flawed encryption algorithms. These attacks can be initiated by hackers to obtain financial information, user passwords, and block legitimate network traffic. A recent example of this was the DDOS attack against Dyn which disrupted websites such as Twitter, Netflix, and Etsy last November.

I have often said that cyberspace is the battlefield of the 21st century. We must act now. Hard-working taxpayers are demanding leadership from Washington in the cyber arena and it is our duty to provide it. Enhanced defensive capabilities should be developed by promoting greater collaboration between public and private entities. CTIA has shown leadership through its Cybersecurity Working Group. Their efforts have brought Federal agencies such as the FCC and DHS together with the private sector to develop solutions to the cybersecurity dilemma.

Whether it is encryption, the use of authentication standards, updating operating systems, or rigorous implementation of antivirus software—we must have an "all of the above" approach when it comes to forging defensive strategies that will defeat and deter cyber criminals.

Thank you and I look forward to the testimony of our witnesses.

Mrs. Blackburn. I thank you all for being here, and at this time I yield 5 minutes to the ranking member, Mr. Doyle.

OPENING STATEMENT OF HON. MICHAEL F. DOYLE, A REPRESENTATIVE IN CONGRESS FROM THE COMMONWEALTH OF PENNSYLVANIA

Mr. Doyle. I thank you, Madam Chair, for holding this hearing and for the witnesses for appearing today. Before I get started I just want to reiterate a momentous occasion in our city. The Pittsburgh Penguins have brought the Stanley Cup back to Pittsburgh for the second year in a row. We beat back broken bones and sideline starters and some ferocious play from the Nashville Predators. I know the Predators aren't squarely in the gentlelady from Tennessee's district, but I want to congratulate her and their team on a hard-fought series.

Mr. McNerney. Will the gentleman yield to someone from the Golden State?

Mr. DOYLE. No. No, I will not. But I have time at the end. You know, in Pittsburgh we could throw Primanti Bros. sandwiches on the ice, but they taste so good we prefer to eat them. So anyways, go Pens and congratulations to the Predators.

I also want to mark another milestone. As of today, there are just under five million comments in the FCC's proceeding to repeal net neutrality rules. With still months to go, we have already far eclipsed the record-breaking 3.7 million comments that were filed in 2015. The vast majority of these comments are overwhelmingly in support of the current rules and opposed to the Trump administration's effort.

And I would once again urge the chairman to bring the Commission before this committee for oversight hearings so that Congress can do its job and provide much needed oversight and public scrutiny. I think it would be a dereliction of duty not to provide oversight of an agency whose actions risk upending the internet ecosystem, one of the primary drivers of our economy.

Considering the number of oversight hearings held during the previous administration, I am sure my colleagues on the other side of the aisle appreciate this fact all too well and will see fit to schedule oversight hearings of the Commission as soon as possible.

Now, on to the topic before us today, promoting online security. Security is an absolutely critical issue. It enables an environment where commerce, communication, and innovation can flourish. However, increasingly, organizations are facing mounting threats and greater challenges particularly as more sectors of our economy come to depend on the digital infrastructure.

These challenges are being compounded by highly sophisticated online threats that are increasingly funded and supported by hostile nations. As the witnesses point out in their testimony, attacks we face today are highly sophisticated and increasingly destructive, from Crash Override to Mirai botnet, from the hacks of the DNC and the Russian meddling in the U.S. election to WannaCry ransomware, these issues are only escalating in their severity.

My colleagues, Representatives Clarke, Engel, and McNerney have all introduced legislation in this committee to address the threats we face. I would encourage the chairman to hold legislative hearings on these bills. I would also add that we need to use every tool in our toolbox to address cyber threats we are facing.

In repealing the FCC's privacy rules using the CRA, Congress also repealed data security protections contained in those rules. While these rules were not a panacea, they required reasonable steps to protect data and were a meaningful step towards addressing this issue.

With that I would yield the remaining minute and 35 seconds of my time to any one of my colleagues that desires to use it. Mr. McNerney?

Mr. MCNERNEY. Well, I thank the ranking member. And I don't want to say too much more about the Golden State Warriors, so I will move on. But I want to thank the Chair for today's hearing.

The security is important. Last October we witnessed a catastrophic attack that used the insecure Internet of Things devices to cripple the internet. A weak device security poses serious threats to our national security and to the economy. That is why I introduced the Securing IoT Act which would require that cybersecurity standards be established for IoT devices and that these devices be certified to meet those standards.

I am also disappointed that my Republican colleagues have not shown any interest in this bill especially since 20 to 50 billion connected devices are expected to be in use by the year 2020. Meanwhile, my Republican colleagues passed the privacy CRA, which leaves consumers more vulnerable to cybersecurity attacks, and that is why I introduced MY DATA Act so that consumers can have strong, data security protections.

I hope my colleagues can get behind these two important bills, and I yield back to the ranking member.

Mr. DOYLE. And Ms. Eshoo, would you like the remaining time?

Ms. ESHOO. Well, you are nice, but there are 11 seconds left, so I will weave my comments in later on. Thank you very much. I appreciate it.

Mr. DOYLE. OK, thank you. I will yield back. Thank you.

Ms. ESHOO. Thank you.

Mrs. BLACKBURN. The gentleman yields back. Mr. Lance, you are recognized for 5 minutes.

OPENING STATEMENT OF HON. LEONARD LANCE, A REPRESENTATIVE IN CONGRESS FROM THE STATE OF NEW JERSEY

Mr. LANCE. Thank you, Chair Blackburn. And welcome to our distinguished panel, thank you for appearing before us today.

Since the advent of the smart phone and network innovations such as 4G LTE, consumers have become increasingly less constrained by location when using the internet. Mobile technology has changed the way consumers interact, freeing them to conduct business, to shop, to have access to health and financial records, to study and participate in countless other activities almost anywhere in the country.

As more and more technological innovations such as 5G and Internet of Things devices come to market, billions more devices will become connected and continue to revolutionize the way consumers and businesses behave. And we have just participated downstairs in a forum regarding the Internet of Things with many of the great companies in this country, including Qualcomm and Panasonic and Siemens and Honeywell and others.

However, with increased ease of access and reliance on connected devices comes increased security risks as the Chair has already indicated. We have already seen bad actors take advantage of the flood of internet-connected devices in the DDOS botnet attacks last year, and an increase of phishing and malware attacks on mobile devices. Threats are constantly evolving and increasing in sophistication and scope.

Cybersecurity needs to be a priority as we become more dependent on connected devices. A large part of this is educating consumers and businesses on how best to protect themselves and their devices on the internet such as recognizing an attempt to invade the internet and regularly to change passwords.

There is also a responsibility for the Government and industry to work together in making sure that networks and consumers are protected without mandating innovation-stifling technology or security standards that will become obsolete quickly. And we have seen this across the last 20 years that technology outstrips what we do here in Washington.

I thank our panel for your efforts in this important field and look forward to the testimony. And I apologize. I will be moving in and out. There are two subcommittees of importance today from the Energy and Commerce Committee. Certainly this is an incredibly important issue and I will certainly be here to the greatest extent possible.

Welcome again to our distinguished panel, and I would yield 2 minutes, 20 seconds to any of our colleagues who wish to be recognized.

Mrs. BLACKBURN. Anyone seeking time for an opening statement? If not, the gentleman yields back.

Mr. LANCE. I yield back, Madam Chair.

Mrs. BLACKBURN. Mr. Pallone, the ranking member of the full committee, you are recognized for 5 minutes.

OPENING STATEMENT OF HON. FRANK PALLONE, JR., A REPRESENTATIVE IN CONGRESS FROM THE STATE OF NEW JERSEY

Mr. PALLONE. Thank you, Madam Chairman.

Cyber attacks are one of the most serious threats to our national security today. Every day, new information comes out about how the Russians and other foreign actors are hacking our institutions and our democracy. Just last week, former FBI Director Comey testified, and I am quoting, "The Russians interfered in our election during the 2016 cycle. They did it with purpose. They did it with sophistication. They did it with overwhelming technical efforts. It was an active measures campaign driven from the top of that government. There is no fuzz on that." Unquote.

This committee has primary jurisdiction over the communications networks that were used by the Russians to commit these attacks. We should be focused like a laser on how to stop them from happening again, but this committee has yet to hold a single hearing on these Russian hacks. Worse still, the only legislation House Republicans have pushed and supported within this subcommittee's jurisdiction actually makes us less safe, in my opinion.

With no hearings or advance notice, the leadership of this committee led the charge to strip away Americans' privacy rights and throw out some of the only protections on the books to secure our data. These safeguards simply said that broadband providers needed to take reasonable measures to secure Americans' data. But despite the Russian hacks, congressional Republicans eliminated those protections under the absurd pretext that asking companies to act reasonably was Government overreach.

This hearing today is another example of committee Republicans simply not taking these issues seriously. Democrats tried to invite another cybersecurity expert to testify here today who could have helped us better understand the threats to our country like the Russian hacks, but the majority made up arbitrary and partisan reasons, in my opinion, to effectively block us. This decision shortchanges our members' ability to hear from the experts in this area.

These games have to stop because these issues are just too serious to keep playing politics with our national security. Now Democrats are trying to address these issues head on in a nonpartisan way. We have put forward three bills—from Mr. Engel, Mr. McNerney, and Ms. Clarke—to help fix some of these problems.

These are good bills that were introduced more than 3 months ago and every day that goes by with no action is another day that the American people are at risk. Republicans, as I said before, should stop playing political games with national security because the risks are too great.

[The prepared statement of Mr. Pallone follows:]

PREPARED STATEMENT OF HON. FRANK PALLONE, JR.

Thank you, Madam Chairman. Cyberattacks are one of the most serious threats to our national security today. Every day new information comes out about how the Russians and other foreign actors are hacking our institutions and our democracy. Just last week former FBI Director Comey testified, and I'm quoting: "The Russians interfered in our election during the 2016 cycle. They did with purpose. They did it with sophistication. They did it with overwhelming technical efforts. It was an active measures campaign driven from the top of that government. There is no fuzz on that."

This committee has primary jurisdiction over the communications networks that were used by the Russians to commit these attacks. We should be focused like a laser on how to stop them from happening again, but this committee has yet to hold a single hearing on these Russian hacks.

Worse still, the only legislation House Republicans have pushed and supported within this subcommittee's jurisdiction actually makes us less safe. With no hearings or advance notice, the leadership of this committee led the charge to strip away Americans' privacy rights and throw out some of the only protections on the books to secure our data.

Those safeguards simply said that broadband providers needed to take "reasonable measures" to secure Americans' data. But despite the Russian hacks, Congressional Republicans eliminated those protections under the absurd pretext that asking companies to act reasonably was Government overreach.

This hearing today is another example of committee Republicans simply not taking these issues seriously. Democrats tried to invite another cybersecurity expert to testify here today who could have helped us better understand the threats to our country, like the Russian hacks. But the majority made up arbitrary and partisan reasons to effectively block us. This decision shortchanges our members' ability to hear from the experts in this area. These games have to stop because these issues are just too serious to keep playing politics with our national security.

Democrats are trying to address these issues head on in a nonpartisan way. We have put forward three bills—from Mr. Engel, Mr. McNerney, and Ms. Clarke—to help fix some of these problems.

These are good bills that were introduced more than three months ago. Every day that goes by with no action is another day that the American people are at risk. Republicans must stop playing political games with national security. The risks are just too great.

Mr. PALLONE. And with that, I would like to yield the time that I have left to Ms. Clarke and Ms. Eshoo. I guess we will split it evenly. We will start, I yield to Ms. Clarke.

Ms. CLARKE. First, I would like to thank our ranking member, Mr. Pallone, for yielding his time to me and thank Ranking Member Doyle and Chairwoman Blackburn for holding this important hearing. And I welcome our witnesses today for their expert testimony, I look forward to hearing from today's panelists.

Many of my constituents in the 9th congressional district of New York have voiced their concerns on cybersecurity and have asked that I and my colleagues what we can do to lessen their vulnerability to cyber attacks which is why I introduced the Cybersecurity Responsibility Act of 2017.

The Cybersecurity Responsibility Act of 2017 calls on the Federal Communications Commission to take an active role in protecting communications networks by carefully arranging, organizing, and supervising cybersecurity risks to prevent cyber attacks. As technology continues to develop and grow, so must our rules and regulations on internet safety. It is our duty not only as Members of Congress but as members of the committee to protect Americans against cyber attacks by ensuring that there are sufficient rules in place. With that, Mr. Chairman, I yield back to you.

Mr. PALLONE. I yield the remaining of the time to Ms. Eshoo.

Ms. ESHOO. I thank the ranking member, and I thank all the witnesses. Some of you have been here before, welcome back, and to those who haven't, welcome.

It has been said but it needs to be restated, cybersecurity, I think, is really one of the most pressing national security issues, challenges for our country. Almost everything that we do here in Congress relative to cybersecurity is after there has been a breach, and I think that we need to really drill down on prevention.

I have spoken to countless people in my Silicon Valley district. Almost to a person they tell me that we need to concentrate on prevention. Up to 90 percent of the breaches, both Government and private sector—and 95 percent of this is private sector, 5 percent is the Federal Government as important as it is—say that there are two pillars to this. One is cyber hygiene and the other is consistent security management, so I am shortly going to be introducing legislation that reflects that.

I think that NIST can set the standards and I think that companies should have a set of good housekeeping seal of approval and that as important as it is to take steps after something has happened, I think that we need to start focusing on prevention.

So we will talk more about it with our distinguished panel, but I want to thank the ranking member for giving me some time to make this brief statement. Thank you.

Mrs. BLACKBURN. The gentlelady yields back. The gentleman yields back, and this concludes our opening statements. I will remind all Members that their opening statements will be made a part of the record.

And we do thank our witnesses for being here with us today. We are going to give each of you the opportunity to make a 5-minute opening statement.

And our witnesses: Mr. Bill Wright who is the director of Government Affairs and Senior Policy Counsel, and we welcome you; Mr. Amit Yoran, who is the chairman and CEO of Tenable; Ms. Kiersten Todt, who is the managing partner at Liberty Group Ventures and a resident scholar at the University of Pittsburgh—I guess you are celebrating too—Institute for Cyber Law, Policy, and Security; and Mr. Charles Clancy, who is the director and professor at Hume Center for National Security and Technology at Virginia Tech.

So we appreciate that you are each here. We will begin, Mr. Wright, with you. You are recognized for 5 minutes for your opening statement.

**STATEMENTS OF BILL WRIGHT, DIRECTOR, GOVERNMENT AF-
FAIRS, AND SENIOR POLICY COUNSEL, SYMANTEC; AMIT
YORAN, CHAIRMAN AND CHIEF EXECUTIVE OFFICER, TEN-
ABLE; CHARLES CLANCY, PH.D., DIRECTOR, HUME CENTER
FOR NATIONAL SECURITY AND TECHNOLOGY, AND PRO-
FESSOR OF ELECTRICAL AND COMPUTER ENGINEERING,
VIRGINIA TECH; AND, KIERSTEN E. TODT, FORMER EXECU-
TIVE DIRECTOR, COMMISSION ON ENHANCING NATIONAL
CYBERSECURITY; MANAGING PARTNER, LIBERTY GROUP
VENTURES, LLC; AND RESIDENT SCHOLAR, UNIVERSITY OF
PITTSBURGH INSTITUTE FOR CYBER LAW, POLICY, AND SE-
CURITY**

STATEMENT OF BILL WRIGHT

Mr. WRIGHT. Chairman Blackburn, Ranking Member Doyle, members of the subcommittee thank you for the opportunity to testify today. The cyber threats that we face today and every day are growing both in numbers and in sophistication. As the chairman pointed out in her opening statement, cyberspace truly is the battlefield of the 21st century.

And while global ransomware attacks and destructive malware attacks tend to steal the headlines, it is other threats—threats to mobile, threats to wireless, threats to IoT—that are quickly gaining prominence. And no wonder, today more than half of the world's web traffic originates from mobile phones and nearly half of the people on the planet own a smart phone today.

But I think calling it a phone doesn't quite do this justice. This isn't a phone. It is a powerful, connected, handheld computer and from time to time you can use it to call your wife. We need to start viewing these as computers and we need to protect them as computers. Our web searches, our banking, our personal health information is all being transmitted and stored on mobile devices. Our smart phones are becoming an extension of ourselves and our identity.

We are also seeing a blurring of the lines between work-issued devices and personal devices. Employees can and often expect to be able to work from anywhere. Workers can unwittingly introduce virus into an entire network system from a single download of a malicious app. IT security is no longer about just protecting the perimeter from attack because that perimeter now covers the entire planet.

As we all rush and rush to connect more and more devices to the internet we will undoubtedly improve our lives in many, many ways, but we will also be greatly increasing the attack surface. Last year's Mirai botnet DDOS attack was a sobering wake-up call for how powerful IoT-based botnet could be. And it was also a chilling reminder for what could happen if those bot masters had trained their sights elsewhere, say on an industrial control system.

Attackers are continuing to evolve their criminal tools and getting better at avoiding detection and obfuscating their actions. The incentives for criminals is very strong. Cybercrime is more lucrative than ever. There is very little risk in getting caught and the underground cybercrime marketplace is booming, allowing even an art history major to conduct highly sophisticated cyber attacks by renting crime as a service by the hour or buying ransomware tool kits or mobile banking trojans.

Mobile device manufacturers, particularly Apple, have done a pretty good job at putting security into their products and keeping malicious apps out of their stores. Android also has made some great strides over the last year. However, the very attributes that make mobile phones so attractive to consumers also make them a very tempting target for cybercriminals because unlike your desktop computer, your mobile device is always active, always receiving and used for every aspect of your life.

Increasingly, smart phones are used for authentication purposes in various online accounts. A hacker only needs to steal or access your mobile device to get past all the other defenses that have been set up on the network side.

Unfortunately, the public's attitude towards securing their devices has not kept pace with the potential threat. More than a quarter of smart phone users do not even use the most basic security feature, the screen lock, let alone applying timely software updates.

And the criminals are following their victims onto these new platforms. Over the last few years we have seen a dramatic rise in malicious activity related to mobile devices driven by cybercriminals using tried and true methods to monetize attacks such as premium text messages, click fraud, and ransomware. Last year, Symantec detected more than 18 million mobile threats, an increase in 105 percent from the prior year. This trend will only be exacerbated over the next few years when tens of billions of connected devices are added to the internet. Cybercriminals are only bound by their own imagination and if there is a way to steal valuable data and monetize it, they will find it.

As this subcommittee knows, we face significant challenges in our efforts to secure wireless networks and mobile devices and while there remains much work to be done we have made some progress in some areas, for instance, how we share threat information and when we share threat information with our Government partners.

At Symantec we are committed to improving online security across the globe, including wireless and mobile security, and will continue to work collaboratively with our customers, industry, and governments to do so. Thank you again for the opportunity to testify and happy to answer any questions.

[The prepared statement of Mr. Wright follows:]

Prepared Testimony and
Statement for the Record of

Bill Wright
Director, Government Affairs & Senior Policy Counsel

Hearing on

"Promoting Security in Wireless Technology"

Before the

United States House of Representatives
Committee on Energy and Commerce
Subcommittee on Communications and Technology

June 13, 2017

Chairman Blackburn, Ranking Member Doyle and members of the Committee, thank you for the opportunity to testify today on behalf of Symantec.

My name is Bill Wright and I am the Director of Government Affairs and Senior Policy Counsel at Symantec, managing a number of global cybercrime and cybersecurity operational relationships. I am responsible for Symantec's global partnership program agenda and government engagement strategy, which includes cybersecurity, data integrity, critical infrastructure protection (CIP), and privacy. In this capacity, I work extensively with industry, government agencies both at home and abroad. Prior to joining Symantec, I was a Staff Director for two U.S. Senate Subcommittees focused on homeland security, government IT and oversight and before that was a Senior Operations Officer at the National Counterterrorism Center Operations Center (NCTC).

Symantec Corporation is the world's leading cybersecurity company, and has the largest civilian threat collection network in the world. Our Global Intelligence NetworkTM tracks over 700,000 global adversaries and is comprised of more than 98 million attack sensors, which record thousands of events every second. This network monitors over 175 million endpoints located in over 157 countries and territories. In addition, we process more than 2 billion emails and over 2.4 billion web requests each day. We maintain nine Security Response Centers and six Security Operations Centers around the globe, and all of these resources combined give our analysts a unique view of the entire cyber threat landscape. Our products and services protect people's information and their privacy across platforms – from the smallest mobile device, to the enterprise data center, to cloud-based systems.

The cyber headlines of the past year have focused on sophisticated state sponsored attacks and global ransomware outbreaks. Cyber attacks are growing both in number and in sophistication. As we move to 5G technologies, billions of new devices will be connected to the Internet, transmitting massive amounts of information and substantially increasing the attack surface. While attacks against traditional desktops and servers have dominated the threat landscape in terms of numbers, there is a growing focus on other platforms, such as wireless networks, IoT, and mobile devices that attackers are now actively targeting.

Wireless devices are now an essential part of our daily lives, and it is essential that they, and the data they contain, remain safe and secure. Understanding the current threat environment is essential if we are going to craft good policy and effective defenses. We are therefore pleased to see the Committee's continued focus on this subject, and appreciate the opportunity to provide our insights.

In my testimony today, I will discuss:

- The Size and Scope of the Cyber Threat Landscape;
- Growing threats across new platforms;
- Mobile threats and best practices; and
- Public-Private Partnerships.

I. The Current and Emerging Cyber Threat Landscape - Overview

Cyber attacks reached new levels in 2016, a year marked by multi-million dollar virtual bank heists, explosive growth of ransomware, attempts to disrupt the US electoral process by state-sponsored groups, a record number of identities exposed in data breaches, and some of the biggest distributed denial of service (DDoS) attacks on record powered by a botnet of Internet of Things (IoT) devices. Yet while the attacks caused unprecedented levels of disruption and financial loss, perhaps the most striking feature of the 2016 attack landscape is that in many cases the attackers used very simple tools and tactics. During 2016, valuable Zero-day vulnerabilities and sophisticated malware was used more sparingly than in recent years. Instead, attackers increasingly attempted to hide in plain sight. They relied on straightforward approaches, such as spear-phishing emails and "living off the land" by using common tools, such as legitimate network administration software and operating system features. Yet despite this trend away from sophisticated attacks, the results were extraordinary, including:

- Over **1.1 billion** identities exposed;
- **Power outages** in the Ukraine;
- Over **$800 million** stolen through Business E-mail Compromise (BEC) scams over just a **six month period**;
- **$81 million** stolen in one bank heist alone;
- A **tripling** of the average ransomware demand;
- Average time-to-attack for a newly connected Internet of Thing device down to **two minutes**.

These shifting tactics demonstrate the resourcefulness of cyber criminals and attackers – but they also show that improved defenses and a concerted effort to address vulnerabilities can make a difference. Attackers are evolving and developing new attacks not because they want to, but because they have to do so. And that evolution comes with a financial cost to the attacker.

Ransomware continues to plague businesses and consumers, and due to its destructiveness is one of the most dangerous cybercrime threats we currently face. During 2016, criminal gangs engaged in indiscriminate campaigns involving massive volumes of malicious emails that in some cases overwhelmed organizations by the sheer volume of ransomware-laden emails alone. Attackers are demanding more and more from victims, and the average ransom demand *more than tripled* in 2016, from $294 to $1,077. The number of new ransomware families also more than tripled to 101, from 30 in both 2014 and 2015. The volume of attacks increased as well. Detections were up 36% percent from 2015, and by December we were seeing almost twice the daily volume that we observed in January.

2016 also saw the emergence of Ransomware-as-a-Service (RaaS). This involves malware developers creating ransomware kits, which can be used easily to create and customize new variants. Typically the developers provide the kits to attackers for a percentage of the proceeds. One example of RaaS is Shark (Ransom.SharkRaaS), which is distributed through its own website and allows users to customize the ransom amount and which files it encrypts. Payment is automated and sent directly to Shark's creators, who retain 20 percent and send the remainder on to the attackers. Our statistics show that, for the most part, attackers are concentrating their attacks on countries with developed, stable economies – 34% of the detections were in the US, and another 39% spread among the United Kingdom, Australia, Germany, Russia, the Netherlands, Canada, India, Italy.

The world of cyber espionage experienced a notable shift towards more overt activity in 2016, much of which was designed to destabilize and disrupt targeted organizations and countries. We saw:

- a January attack against the Ukrainian power grid;
- an attack on the World Anti-Doping Agency and subsequent release of test results;
- a widespread, destructive attack on computers in Saudi Arabia; and

- a second attack against the Ukrainian power grid in December.

In years past, any one of these events would have been the biggest story of the year. But in 2016, we also saw an attack on the US Presidential election, an operation that the Intelligence Community (IC) attributed to Russia. Cyber attacks involving sabotage have traditionally been rare, but 2016 saw two separate waves of attacks involving destructive malware. Disk-wiping malware was used against targets in the attacks on the Ukraine in January and again in December, resulting in power outages. Additionally, a disk-wiping trojan known as Shamoon reappeared after a four-year absence and was used against multiple organizations in Saudi Arabia. Previously, Shamoon was used in highly destructive attacks against Saudi and other Middle Eastern energy companies, and press reports linked it to Iran.

In 2016, cyber criminals expanded their focus from individual bank customers to the banks themselves, sometimes attempting to steal tens of millions of dollars in a single attack. Two groups targeted the Society for Worldwide Interbank Financial Telecommunication (SWIFT) network and stole SWIFT credentials. They used those credentials to initiate fraudulent transactions and covered their tracks by doctoring the banks' printed confirmation messages to delay discovery of the transfers. One group began its attack at the start of a long weekend to reduce the likelihood of a quick discovery.

Good security does not happen by accident – it requires planning and continued attention. But criminals will always be evolving and adapting, and security must as well.

II. Growing threats Across New Platforms

And while ransomware and financial fraud groups continue to pose the biggest threat to individual users, other threats are beginning to emerge. It was only a matter of time before attacks on IoT devices began to gain momentum, and during 2016 Symantec witnessed a twofold increase in attempted attacks against IoT devices. 2016 also saw the first major incident originating from IoT devices, the Mirai botnet, which was composed of routers, digital video cameras, and security cameras. Weak security – in the form of default and hard-coded passwords – made these devices easy pickings for attackers. After compromising millions of devices, the attackers controlled a botnet big enough to carry out the largest DDoS attacks ever seen. In October, the combined power of these compromised devices led to brief outages at some of the most popular websites and online services in the world. Mirai's impact was further magnified when the developer released the source code for the malware, which led to copycat efforts by other groups.[1]

Though there is no single way to fix a complex problem like this, risk-based baseline security standards are part of the solution. Of course, manufacturers should take the lead role in the security of the products that they are sending to market. They should provide consumers a level of transparency in the security of connected devices so that consumers can make informed decisions. This also allows security to become an inherent feature of a device, which would allow premium manufacturers to differentiate their products based on security.

As cloud usage by both enterprises and consumers has become mainstream, attackers have increased their focus on it. While cloud attacks are still in their infancy, last year we saw the first widespread outage of cloud services as a result of a denial of service (DoS) campaign, serving as a warning for how susceptible cloud services are to malicious activity. Widespread adoption of cloud applications in

---

[1] See *Symantec Internet Security Threat Report*, XXII, April 2017 pp. 68

corporations, coupled with risky user behavior that the corporation may not even be aware of, creates new opportunities for cloud-based attacks.

Part of this is because many organizations simply do not understand how much they rely on the cloud. At the end of 2016, the average enterprise organization was using 928 cloud apps, up from 841 earlier in the year. However, our research found that most CIOs believed that their organizations were using only 30 to 40 cloud apps. Attackers, on the other hand, grasp the opportunity for mischief and crime in the cloud - during 2015, we identified more than 3 million malicious apps that were in fact malware, which was nearly 30% of all apps that were analyzed. Most of these malicious apps were from third party app stores.[2]

III. Mobile Threats

With billions of smartphones and tablets and tens billions of Internet-connected devices coming on line, the focus of Internet security must shift from the desktop to the pocket, the purse, and the home. Today more than half of the world's population uses a smartphone and more than half of the world's web traffic now originates from mobile phones.[3] In the United States, these trends are even higher. People are using their mobile devices in nearly every aspect of their lives – from accessing their bank accounts, to sensitive health and business activity, to conducting e-commerce. The lines are quickly blurring between what constitutes a work device and a personal device. Our mobile devices are filled with valuable personal and business related data, and more often than not, the information stored on a mobile device is worth far more than the device itself.

Unfortunately, the very attributes that make mobile devices attractive to consumers also make them an enticing target for cybercriminals. Criminals use a number of techniques to steal or otherwise monetize your information including, phishing, malware, and ransomware. These threats are evolving and becoming more sophisticated. Cybercriminals are bound only by their imagination.

Mobile Malware: The number of malware detections on mobile devices doubled in 2016 to more than 18 million. Cybercriminals continue to employ mobile malware primarily for financial theft and fraud, using tried and true monetization methods, such as stealing user account credentials (i.e. banking), sending premium text messages, advertisement click-fraud, and ransomware. Infections can occur in a number of ways – from downloading a malicious applications to visiting an infected website. Malware targeting financial institutions and their customers have focused on mobile users more often in the last year. In response, financial institutions have increased their security measures in their interactions with customers and also on their own backend systems. However, cybercriminals are adapting and mimicking the customer's behavior as closely as possible and attacking the institution themselves. Since the introduction of mobile banking apps and two-factor authentication (2FA), cyber criminals have had to look for ways to either bypass 2FA using social engineering or by attacking the mobile device itself. 2FA is an added security authentication tool that requires not only a password and username but also something that only the user would know or have access to.[4]

---

[2] https://www.symantec.com/content/dam/symantec/docs/reports/istr-21-2016-en.pdf

[3] https://www.slideshare.net/wearesocialsg/digital-in-2017-global-overview

[4] https://www.symantec.com/content/dam/symantec/docs/security-center/white-papers/istr-financial-threats-review-2017-en.pdf

Mobile Ransomware: Ransomware has dominated the threat landscape for the last two years and has achieved mainstream notoriety with the May 12th global outbreak of the WannaCry Ransomware. WannaCry hit more than 300,00 victims in 150 countries, and crippled Britain's National Health Services and other critical sectors.[5] Criminals are taking lessons they learned from traditional ransomware attacks on PCs and applying them to mobile platforms. Like its PC counterpart, mobile ransomware infects your device and encrypts sensitive data, and then demands payment, often via Bitcoin, in exchange for unlocking or returning you data. Mobile ransomware most often masquerades itself as a legitimate app, usually in a third party app store. In many ways, mobile devices are more integrated into our daily lives than our PCs ever were, and as a result mobile ransomware can have a devastating impact on consumers and business alike.

Mobile Phishing: The popularity of mobile devices has made them a frequent target of traditional web-based attacks, especially phishing.[6] Phishing is another example of how tried and true PC-based attacks have been adapted to mobile platforms. Phishing is not a new attack, and is rooted in social engineering – aiming to trick the user into doing something they would never do if they were fully aware of the dangers. In a traditional, PC based phishing attack if a criminal wanted to steal your banking credentials he would compose an email or a social media posting to lure the victim to a fake website, designed to look legitimate. There, the unwitting victim would use his log-on credentials, passing them onto the cybercriminal. However, mobile users are far less likely to log into their bank through a web browser, so the savvy criminal phishes through malicious apps. Mobile apps are self-contained tools and enjoy a higher level of trust. While phishing apps are a new take on an old theme, they are highly effective at stealing your information.

Public-Private Partnerships

The growing challenge of securing the mobile environment will require more than just increased user awareness. It will take participation from all of the mobile communication stakeholders – ISPs, device manufacturers, software developers, security vendors, government, consumers, and enterprises to help secure the mobile ecosystem. Symantec partners closely with governments to help identify threat trends, share threat information, develop innovative security tools, and publish best practices.

Some partnership programs are formal, such as the Cyber Information Sharing and Collaboration Program (CISCP). This is DHS's primary structure for private companies to share information about incidents, cyber threats and known vulnerabilities. For example, last October, we used the CISCP program to share a report we published that exposed one of the groups that was trying to steal money from banks by exploiting the SWIFT messaging system. Through CISCP, we passed along our in-depth, technical research to CISCP managers along with a list of indicators including hashes, command and control nodes, and domains. The CISCP team then used our indicators to create an Indicator Bulletin (IB) and pushed it out to all CISCP participants for their use.

Partnerships can lead to concrete results. One recent example came in December 2016, when Symantec concluded a decade-long research campaign that helped unearth an international cybercriminal gang dubbed "Bayrob." The group is responsible for stealing up to $35 million from victims through auto auction scams, credit card fraud and computer intrusions. Through our research, we discovered multiple versions of Bayrob malware, collected voluminous intelligence data, and tracked Bayrob as it

---

[5] https://www.symantec.com/connect/blogs/what-you-need-know-about-wannacry-ransomware
[6] http://www.csoonline.com/article/3103296/mobile-security/mobile-phishing-same-attacks-different-hooks.html

morphed from online fraud to a botnet consisting of over 300,000 computers used primarily for cryptocurrency mining. Over time, Symantec's research team gained deep technical insight into Bayrob's operations and its malicious activities, including its recruitment of money mules. These investigations and countermeasures were crucial in assisting the Federal Bureau of Investigation (FBI) and authorities in Romania in building their case to arrest three of Bayrob's key actors and extradite them to the U.S. They are currently in federal custody awaiting trial.

The private sector is also working together to counter cybercrime and industry partnerships have proven highly effective in fighting cybercrime. The Cyber Threat Alliance (CTA) is an excellent example of the private sector banding together to improve the overall safety and security of the Internet. In 2014, Symantec, Fortinet, Intel Security, and Palo Alto Networks formed the CTA to work together to share threat information, including mobile threats. Since that time, Cisco and Checkpoint have joined the CTA as founding members. The goal of the CTA is to better distribute detailed information about advanced attacks and thereby raise the situational awareness of CTA members and improve overall protection for our customers. Prior industry sharing efforts were often limited to the exchange of malware samples, and the CTA sought to change that. Over the past three years the CTA has consistently shared more actionable threat intelligence such as information on "zero day" vulnerabilities, command and control server information, mobile threats, and indicators of compromise related to advanced threats. By raising the industry's collective intelligence through these new data exchanges, CTA members have delivered greater security for individual customers and organizations.[7]

Conclusion

At Symantec, we work hard to educate consumers by providing guidelines to protect personal data on the Internet. There are a number of basic things that consumers can do to protect themselves from common mobile threats. First and foremost, both consumers and employers should begin treating mobile devices like the small, powerful, computers that they are, including:

- Regularly patch and update your software.
- Do not download apps from unfamiliar sites.
- Use different passwords for different apps.
- Pay close attention to the permissions being requested by apps.
- Install security on your mobile devices.
- Make frequent backups of important data.
- Be vigilant for phishing schemes.

Effectively defending networks and devices will require continuous innovation. As our wireless networks move to 5G technologies, we will be connecting more and more devices to the Internet and transferring previously unimaginable amounts of data. The trust in the Internet will hinge on how secure that data, those devices, and those networks can be made. We are pleased to assist the Committee as it examines these issues.

---

[7] https://cyberthreatalliance.org

Mrs. BLACKBURN. I thank you for the testimony.

Mr. Yoran, you are recognized for 5 minutes.

STATEMENT OF AMIT YORAN

Mr. YORAN. Chairman Blackburn, Ranking Member Doyle, and members of the subcommittee thank you for the opportunity to testify today in what promises to be the most exciting hearing of the day. I am chairman and CEO of Tenable, the world's most widely deployed vulnerability management solution including in the Federal Government where the majority of Government agencies use our technology to assess and manage their cyber risk.

It is important to put mobility and wireless in the context of modern computing enterprise environments which are dynamic and borderless and virtually unlimited in connectivity. Mobile devices, wireless networks, transient user populations, cloud-based infrastructure, web applications, and the shift to DevOps go hand in glove with the Internet of Things in invading our computing environments.

Today's complex mix of computer platforms and applications combine to represent the modern attack surface where the assets themselves and their associated vulnerabilities are constantly expanding, contracting, and evolving, almost like a living organism, creating gaps in overall system understanding, security coverage, and resulting in underestimated exposure. Therefore, it is important that any approach to cybersecurity for mobile devices or wireless networks not be done in isolation but, rather, viewed as part of a holistic ecosystem.

In over 20 years practicing information security, the following axiom proves true time and again. You cannot secure what you don't know about. If there are elements of your computing environment that are invisible or unknown to you, chances are that they represent unaccounted-for risk.

Both the NIST Cybersecurity Framework and DHS's Continuous Diagnostics and Mitigation program call for identifying assets and vulnerabilities as the first step in cybersecurity. Identifying assets not just once but continually is foundation to assessing risk and developing effective security programs. My written testimony includes policy recommendations, a few of which I will highlight.

First, we need a bold, new cyber workforce strategy that develops and advances the ranks of all people from different walks of life. Only through increased inclusion and diversity in perspective and thought can our industry achieve the greater creativity, innovation, and develop new solutions to our most vexing challenges.

At Tenable we have implemented a Rooney Rule to set an example of greater diversity in our leadership ranks. I do want to state, however, that our efforts to expand the workforce will inevitably fall short of the insatiable demand for cyber talent and we have to prepare for that with a complementary focus on technology and automation.

Second, the Government should encourage the private-sector companies to continually and fully assess their cybersecurity risk just as the Federal agencies will be doing and many regulatory requirements and best practices already mandate. Today, all organi-

zations are part of a global ecosystem with a cyber hygiene responsibility to one another.

Simple malware like WannaCry demonstrated what a very crippling cyber attack might do. The infection was spread company to
company, many of which simply failed to adequately assess their
cyber risk and act accordingly. Third, the Federal Government
should continue to promote the NIST Cybersecurity Framework
which, according to Gartner, will be adopted by 50 percent of organizations by 2020.

In closing, I want to emphasize the importance of taking an
agile, continuous, and holistic approach to cybersecurity and technology policy. As we all know, IT is changing quickly across so
many different dimensions. Prudence would have us look at mobile
devices, wireless networks, and other technologies gaining great
adoption in the broader context of our IT environments rather than
in isolation.

I would like to thank Chairman Blackburn, Ranking Member
Doyle, and all the members of the subcommittee for their attention
to this important issue and I will be happy to respond to your questions.

[The prepared statement of Mr. Yoran follows:]

Written Testimony
Amit Yoran
Chairman and CEO, Tenable
House Energy and Commerce Committee
Communications and Technology Subcommittee
"Promoting Security in Wireless Technology"
June 13, 2017

Introduction

Chairman Blackburn, Ranking Member Doyle, and members of the Subcommittee, thank you for the opportunity to testify today on promoting security in wireless technology. The security of mobile devices and wireless networks is a critical aspect in the overall cybersecurity posture of not only the federal government, but also private businesses and consumers everywhere, and I applaud the Committee's efforts to better understand all aspects of this issue.

My name is Amit Yoran and I am the Chairman and CEO of Tenable. I have spent over 20 years in the cybersecurity field. I received a Master of Science in computer science from the George Washington University and a Bachelor of Science in computer science from the United States Military Academy. I served as the National Cyber Security Director from 2003-2004 and as the founding Director of the US-CERT program. Additionally, I have served on a number of Presidential advisory commissions. As an innovator and entrepreneur in the security space, I founded and built two security companies: Riptech, acquired by Symantec; and NetWitness, acquired by RSA, where I went on to serve as the president of RSA from 2014 through 2016. I have also served as a director and advisor to security startups and industry advisory boards. I have previously testified before congressional committees on cybersecurity policy, encryption and other related issues.

The company I lead, Tenable, is based in nearby Columbia, Maryland. Tenable has 900 employees globally, more than 23,000 customers worldwide, and more than one million global users. We are the world's leading provider of vulnerability assessment technology. Our company is focused on transforming security technology through comprehensive solutions that provide continuous visibility and critical context, enabling decisive actions that help our customers protect their respective organizations from growing cyber threats. Our goal is to eliminate blind spots, prioritize threats and reduce exposure and loss.

Simply put, Tenable empowers organizations of all sizes to understand and reduce their cybersecurity risk. This includes the federal government, where Tenable provides the most widely deployed vulnerability management solution.

The Elastic Attack Surface

The modern enterprise environment is dynamic and borderless, with virtually unlimited connectivity. Employees bring personal devices to work, contractors use their computers on corporate networks, and people connect to new cloud instances daily. IT teams spin up virtual machines and services to meet demand, and create and connect microservices-based containers on the fly, decommissioning them just as fast; a process commonly referred to as elastic computing. These mobilization and digitization trends foster a boon in productivity and create agility for the modern enterprise. This is all done while IT teams manage the on-site and legacy architectures, which have been invaded by a slew of enterprise network attached Internet of Things (IoT) devices, including TVs, thermostats, motion sensors, locks, webcams, shades and other control systems to name just a few. According to Business Insider's research service, by 2019 there will be 23.3 billion IoT devices, forty percent (40%) of which will be enterprise IoT devices. These 9.1 billion devices will effectively reside on enterprise wireless networks, representing more than the smartphone and tablet market in their entirety (projected to increase to 6 billion by 2019).[1]

For the first time, concern about IoT security ranked higher in ISACA's State of Cyber Security member survey than concerns about losing mobile devices. Only 13 percent of respondents cited lost mobile devices as an exploitation vector in 2016, compared to 34 percent in 2015. By contrast, 30 percent in 2016 said they were either "extremely" or "very concerned" about IoT in the workplace, with 29 percent saying they were "concerned."[2]

Today's complex mix of computer platforms and environments varies by system longevity, location, manageability, importance and function, yet they combine to represent today's modern attack surface, where the assets themselves and their associated vulnerabilities are constantly expanding, contracting and evolving like a living organism, creating gaps in overall system understanding, security coverage and resulting in exposure.

Nevertheless, mobile device threats still warrant concern. A problem facing many organizations,

---

[1] Business Insider, "The corporate 'Internet of Things' will encompass more devices than the smartphone and tablet markets combined," http://www.businessinsider.com/the-enterprise-internet-of-things-market-2014-12
[2] ISACA, "State of Cybersecurity 2017," http://www.isaca.org/Knowledge-Center/Research/Documents/state-of-cybersecurity-2017-part-2_res_eng_0517.PDF?regnum=376901

including government, is the workforce using multiple mobile devices – smartphones, tablets, laptops – some of which are owned by the organization, and many of which belong to individuals. To boost productivity, increasingly each of them needs to be able to access organizational networks and resources. This presents several problems, including not knowing who is using which device, whether the devices have the latest software updates, or if device has been tampered with (i.e., jailbroken). Another challenge with mobile devices is their unpredictability: they hop from cellular 3G to 4G to corporate wireless networks seamlessly and are turned off and on at various times.

While still less common than malware targeting desktops, there is an increase in malware specifically designed for mobile devices. Malware attacks against smartphones rose nearly 400 percent in 2016, according to Nokia's 2017 Threat Intelligence Report.[3] Smartphones were the most targeted devices in the second half of the year, the report finds, accounting for 85 percent of all mobile device infections. Security issues pertaining to mobile devices are growing aggressively. Particularly troubling is the rise of nasty "rootkit" malware being distributed to mobile phones via various online stores. This type of malware is quickly rivaling its desktop counterparts in complexity, with sophisticated control of its host, the ability to hide and prevent easy removal.[4]

Vulnerabilities of Wireless Networks

In addition to risks posed by mobile devices, wireless networks present their own set of security challenges. Content traversing wireless networks can frequently be eavesdropped even if it appears to be encrypted. This is a warning that security-conscious consumers should heed.

Organizations frequently add wireless access points (WAPs) to their network to free user laptops and computers from network cables and reduce data charges incurred by cellular carriers. Sometimes organizations have security policies prohibiting wireless access points – but that doesn't mean that others don't add them on their own, a practice referred to as rogue wireless access points.

It's also possible to surreptitiously create a wireless access point on a network. Attackers can configure a WAP so that it appears identical to an organization's actual wireless network. This phenomenon is sometimes known as creating an "evil twin."[5] If an evil twin hits the mark and is

---

[3] Nokia, "Nokia Threat Intelligence Report 2H 2016," https://pages.nokia.com/8859.Threat.Intelligence.Report.html
[4] International Business Times, "More than 50,000 Android devices may be infected with dangerous 'Dvmap' malware," http://www.ibtimes.co.uk/more-50000-android-devices-may-be-infected-dangerous-dvmap-malware-1625548

[5] SecurityMetrics.com, "Wireless Access Point Protection: Finding Rogue Wi-Fi Networks," http://blog.securitymetrics.com/2016/03/wireless-access-point-protection.html

mistaken for the organization's wireless network, an authorized user might connect to it, allowing attackers access to the user's device and where they can steal authentication credentials and access the network seamlessly. Whether it's an employee or an attacker, or even a piece of malware converting a laptop or other device so that it behaves as a WAP, the effect is that network administrators have lost visibility into the security of that wireless environment, and its impact on the network.

The potential significance of wireless networks is increasing with the addition of IoT devices, which often communicate over wireless. When we talk about the security implications of IoT, we have to think not only about securing the devices themselves, but also the wireless networks on which they operate.

While initial implementation efforts might segregate IoT from enterprise traffic, this is a trend that will likely not be defensible over time, as the desired interaction between people and devices includes the sharing of all kinds of data with each other wirelessly, mandating that sensor, beacons, senders and receivers can seamlessly communicate. Already we have seen sensitive networks hosting industrial control systems connected to enterprise data networks for convenience of administration, where they were formerly segregated onto private "air-gapped" networks.

Methods for creating rogue access points and intercepting traffic holds just as true for cellular networks and the phone conversations and data that they carry. These techniques have been known for years and are readily found. Unidentified signal carriers have been discovered near US military bases.[6] Rogue cellular signals don't require a massive cell tower or a PhD to create. For $25, you can build one on a cheap, portable and inconspicuous Rasberry Pi.[7]

There are a number of easy to use applications that can provide end to end encryption and protect data and voice communications while using smartphones, such as Wickr, Signal, and TrustCall. These technologies can provide protection, even when communicating over untrusted networks.

There are a number of technologies to help secure mobile devices, such as VMWare's AirWatch, and other mobile device management (MDM) solutions. Even some cloud-based providers include basic device management and the ability to provide some protection to your data once it's moved onto a mobile platform. These capabilities frequently include enabling remote wipe, turning on encryption, or setting complex passcodes. There are also technologies that are capable of defining how mobile devices can access your information, who is using them, and if the devices contain vulnerabilities. Mobile security has quickly become a non-negotiable part of any organization's security program, but it should not be done in isolation.

---

[6] Popular Science, "Mysterious Phony Cell Towers Could Be Intercepting Your Calls,"
http://www.popsci.com/article/technology/mysterious-phony-cell-towers-could-be-intercepting-your-calls
[7] PhoneArena.com, "DIY enthusiasts make their own cell phone tower using a Raspberry Pi,"
http://www.phonearena.com/news/DIY-enthusiasts-make-their-own-cell-phone-tower-using-a-Raspberry-Pi_id37976

Solution: Know Your Network

It is critical to recognize that the diversity of the modern compute environment includes on premise servers and computers, wireless, mobile, IoT, cloud, web apps, and containers. And it's equally important to not take a siloed approach to mobile security or any other aspect of security, but rather view it as part of the holistic ecosystem. As with mobile and the broader ecosystem, the following axiom proves true time and again; you can't secure what you do not know. If there are elements of your modern computing environment that you don't have visibility into, chances are they represent misunderstood and unaccounted-for risk.

The highly regarded NIST Cybersecurity Framework validates this. The Framework lays out five essential functions for every cybersecurity effort: identify, protect, detect, respond, and recover. There's a reason the first function is to "identify": You can't successfully implement the other four steps without first knowing what is on your modern compute environment. Likewise, the Continuous Diagnostics and Mitigation (CDM) program, organized by DHS for civilian government agencies, takes a similar approach. According to DHS,

> CDM provides federal departments and agencies with capabilities and tools that identify cybersecurity risks on an ongoing basis, prioritize these risks based upon potential impacts, and enable cybersecurity personnel to mitigate the most significant problems first.

You have to be able to identify assets, so that you can assess risk. You have to know your network and systems – just as an attacker maps out a network before launching an exploit. And knowing your network is more than just the first step in a cybersecurity exercise; it has to be a continuous step, especially as the compute base changes and your attack surface continues to morph indefinitely.

In one example from the PC world, the recent WannaCry and related ransomware attacks could have been prevented if organizations had known their systems, the associated high-profile vulnerabilities and patched them in a timely manner. Continuous visibility into the existence and vulnerability of every asset in the modern computing environment – including mobile devices and wireless networks – is critical to understanding the business impact of any attack. Knowing your network and its vulnerabilities at all times is part of good cyber hygiene, which the Center for Internet Security says consists of five actions: Count, Configure, Control, Patch and Repeat. Again, the first order of business is to count – identify, scan, enumerate, map, or know what is out there. Without that step, the cybersecurity efforts are far less likely to be effective.

Policy Recommendations

I'd also like to offer some policy recommendations that I believe would help secure networks, including wireless, as well as enhance cybersecurity practices.

First, there is a well-documented shortage in the cybersecurity workforce. In order to solve the cybersecurity challenges we face today, we need to make sure we are recruiting, developing and maintaining the best talent. According to the Global Information Security Workforce Study (GISWS) released in February, the workforce shortage is projected to reach 1.8 million people by 2022.[8] Women constitute only 14% of the cybersecurity workforce in North America and just 11% of the cyber workforce globally.

It is up to industry, along with Congress, to increase accountability and reduce this gap. We need a bold, new cyber workforce strategy that develops and advances the ranks of people from all walks of life. While the private sector can lead the way, we need buy-in and partnership from the government.

I know many companies are actively working with the government to address the cybersecurity workforce shortage, but the workforce strategy depends on more than a willingness to change. We must think innovatively and revisit our approach to attracting and retaining talent. Management and leadership courses should be made more inclusive to diversity. Only through increased inclusion and diversity in perspective and thought, can our industry achieve greater creativity, innovation, and develop new solutions to our most vexing challenges. At Tenable, we have implemented a "Rooney Rule" and are setting an example of greater diversity in our leadership ranks.

I do want to state, however, that our efforts to expand the human workforce will inevitably fall short of the insatiable and growing demand for cyber talent, and we have to prepare for that. We need to have a complementary focus on technology and automation so that we can make the most of the human experts we have. Asymmetric leverage of our cyber talent through the use of technology is the only path to success.

Second, the Administration recently released the Cybersecurity Executive Order, which specifically calls out the importance of securing critical infrastructure. The government should encourage private sector companies to continually fully assess their cybersecurity risk, just as federal agencies will be doing and some regulatory requirements and best practices already mandate.

This is an important step forward, and even more still needs to be done. Today all organizations

---

[8] The Center for Cyber Safety and Education and the Executive Women's Forum on Information Security, Risk Management and Privacy, "The 2017 Global Information Security Workforce Study: Women in Cybersecurity," https://iamcybersafe.org/wp-content/uploads/2017/03/WomensReport.pdf

are part of a global ecosystem and have a cyber hygiene responsibility to one another. This can be thought of using vaccination as an analogy. Simple malware like WannaCry demonstrated what a crippling attack in the future might do. As a result, you had factories closing like Renault in France, hospitals refusing patients such as NHS in the UK, and numerous other examples. While not blaming the victims, the infection was spread company-to-company, many of which simply failed to adequately assess and address their cybersecurity risk.

In some instances patching systems isn't possible or practical. This may be true, but it doesn't alleviate the fundamental responsibility to understand risk and apply appropriate compensating controls or other countermeasures.

In commercial cases this shared responsibility extends to customers and shareholders, and in governments' case, to their citizens. I am not advocating a mandate for some elusive perfect security, but simply stating that good cyber hygiene is in our individual enterprise and global ecosystem's best interest.

Third, in order to see and protect assets, including mobile devices, the federal government should support a modern approach to cybersecurity that is based not only on scanning, but discovery of unknown assets and assessing their vulnerability. With the right technology, agencies can gain real-time visibility into their asset base and where they are exposed, and the insight to help prioritize the risks that matter most. Without such an enlightened and proactive approach, government agencies will never be able to answer the most fundamental questions in security: where and how am I exposed? And what can I do to most efficiently reduce my risk? To reiterate the learnings of the NIST Framework and CDM program, the process starts with a deep knowledge of your systems and their exposures.

Fourth, the federal government can promote the establishment and adoption of best practices by encouraging engagements such as the NIST Cybersecurity Framework. A product of various stakeholders, the Framework has been widely praised and, according to Gartner, will be adopted by 50 percent of organizations by 2020.[9] This public-private initiative is achieving adoption because it's a voluntary, industry-led program that makes sense. It offers a prioritized, flexible, repeatable, and cost-effective approach for enterprise leadership to understand cybersecurity risk. Its recommendations are accessible to cybersecurity professionals and other organizational stakeholders. The federal government should continue to support the NIST Cybersecurity Framework and other efforts to create guidance for improved cybersecurity. One such piece of guidance could be around automated asset discovery for both private and public-sector organizations, fulfilling one of the tenants of the Framework.

---

[9] Intrinium.com, "NIST Cybersecurity Framework: Adoption or Bust!" https://intrinium.com/nist-cybersecurity-framework-adoption-or-bust/

Finally, it's worth mentioning the recent legislation relating to IT modernization. It is promising to see Congress rallying behind much-needed measures such as the Modernizing Government Technology Act (MGT Act), sponsored by Representatives Will Hurd and Gerry Connolly. While this legislation involves all systems, not just wireless devices, it represents a meaningful step in the right direction toward providing adequate, risk-based, and cost-effective information technology capabilities that address evolving threats to information security.

Closing

In closing, I want to emphasize the importance of taking an agile, continuous and holistic approach to cybersecurity and technology policy. As we all know, IT is changing quickly along so many dimensions. We should take great care to not consider any aspect of IT in a silo, but rather embed security as an integral part of initiatives where IT assets and connected devices are deployed. Wireless networks are an important part of our technology ecosystem – especially with IoT devices coming online at fantastic rates. Let's look at wireless networks in the broader context of our agile IT environments, the elastic attack surface and the broader ecosystem of internet technology.

I would like to thank Chairman Blackburn and Ranking Member Doyle and all the members of the Subcommittee for their attention to this important issue. I appreciate the opportunity to be here today and look forward to working with you and your colleagues as cybersecurity topics remain at the forefront of so many policy decisions we face. I will be happy to respond to your questions.

Mrs. BLACKBURN. I thank the gentleman and he yields back and, Dr. Clancy, you are recognized for 5 minutes.

STATEMENT OF CHARLES CLANCY

Dr. CLANCY. Thank you, Chairman Blackburn, Ranking Member Doyle, and subcommittee members. I think we can all agree that there are major vulnerabilities in the larger ecosystem of wireless security that we have reason to be concerned about. I would like to focus my opening remarks a bit on the wireless infrastructure that underpins those networks.

Over the last decade we have seen a fundamental shift of the DNA of the internet from the internet that connected stationary computers to fixed server infrastructure to one that is the social mobile internet. It is ubiquitous mobile broadband that connects smart phones and users to social media and the internet as a whole.

This has again fundamentally changed the makeup of the traffic on the internet and the nature of the cybersecurity threat to the internet. Over the next decade we will see another titanic shift of the internet with the so-called Internet of Things which has been referred by several others so far, but the idea here is that we could see an increase of 20 billion devices connected to the internet; again another fundamental titanic shift of the DNA of the internet.

The wireless industry is working aggressively to address the needs of IoT with 5G wireless technology and is seeking to make sure that there are security components that are built into the infrastructure to address those needs. If you look at our cellular infrastructure today, the majority of us have 4G LTE coverage.

And 4G LTE learned from the mistakes of 3G, which learned from the mistakes of 2G, which learned from the mistakes of 1G, and for the most part has the needed building blocks to develop and manage a secure, wireless, mobile broadband infrastructure. The key challenge we have though is that while 4G LTE is ubiquitously deployed, we still have 2G and 3G infrastructure that is operating, and much of the rest of the world has 2G and 3G infrastructure operating that remains vulnerable to a wide range of different attacks.

And in particular, in the last 12 months we have seen press around IMSI catchers or so-called StingRays that are able to compromise user privacy and the SS7 attacks that were able to impact user privacy as well. And the big challenge is not that 4G LTE is insecure, it is just that we still have this legacy 2G infrastructure deployed that remains insecure.

Additionally, we have unlicensed bands, unlicensed technology, wireless technology-fueled innovation over the last decade or two, right. WiFi fundamentally transformed many aspects of how we connect to the internet and how internet is available to us. However, in the early days of WiFi there were rampant security vulnerabilities. My Ph.D. dissertation was studying those vulnerabilities and looking to address them in the standards that ultimately became WPA and WPA2, which ultimately shored up many of those vulnerabilities.

And while home users and residential WiFi networks are for the most part secure through deployment of these new technologies, hotspots at everywhere from your coffee shop to airplanes remain insecure and are vulnerable to attacks that we have known about for 2 decades. So that remains, I think, a challenge as we look at the wireless ecosystem as a whole.

Third, I would look at the services that operate over these networks, right. We have a very complex tapestry of members of this ecosystem. We have the device manufacturers, we have the operating system vendors, we have the people who write and develop apps that run on these systems. We have the cellular operators. We have the OEMs who build equipment for the cellular operators. We have the cloud providers and we have the median service entities that sit over top of all of it. And each of one of these different groups has a different regulatory focal point within the U.S. Government, whether it be the Federal Communications Commission or the Federal Trade Commission or DHS, and this creates a very complex ecosystem when seeking to achieve cybersecurity because no one entity across that entire continuum has enough control of the ecosystem to achieve unilateral security.

So as a result, I think it is imperative that we look at cybersecurity as a partnership where we need stakeholders across all the, both Government and industry to be working together on developing solutions and deploying those solutions.

And lastly, as a member of the academic community, I will reinforce the points that have been made earlier around workforce. There are over a million cybersecurity jobs here in the United States of which 31 percent are vacant. The number of new jobs in cybersecurity each year that become open exceeds the total volume of computer scientists graduating across the entire United States.

So we need to think more broadly about how we fill these cybersecurity gaps, and we need to think of cybersecurity not just as a subdiscipline of computer science, but something that is fundamentally intrinsic to technology overall. And with that I will thank the chairman and conclude my remarks.

[The prepared statement of Mr. Clancy follows:]

Testimony of Dr. Charles Clancy

Professor of Electrical and Computer Engineering, Virginia Tech

before the House Energy and Commerce Committee, Subcommittee on Communications and Technology, Hearing on Promoting Security in Wireless Technologies

June 13, 2017

Introduction

Chairman Blackburn, Ranking Member Doyle, and Subcommittee Members:

My name is Charles Clancy and I am a professor of electrical and computer engineering at Virginia Tech, where I direct the Hume Center for National Security and Technology. In these roles, I lead major university programs in cybersecurity and telecommunications. I am an internationally-recognized expert in wireless security and have held leadership roles within international standards and technology organizations including the Internet Engineering Task Force (IETF) and Institute of Electrical and Electronics Engineers (IEEE). From 2015-2016 I led the successful negotiations between the Pentagon and wireless industry on security requirements for spectrum sharing in the Navy's 3.5 GHz radar band, and from 2008-2012 I led the development of security requirements for military deployment of WiMAX, LTE, and cognitive radio technologies. I am co-author to over 200 peer-reviewed academic publications, to include five books on digital communications; am co-inventor to over 20 patents; and am co-founder of four venture-back startup companies all focused in the wireless and security sectors. Prior to joining Virginia Tech in 2010, I served as research leader for emerging mobile technologies at the National Security Agency.

Background

While viewed as a luxury a few decades ago, access to wireless communications is a critical component of our society. Over the past decade, smartphones have further entrenched our reliance on wireless communications and the need for ubiquitous mobile broadband. The next decade brings the so-called Internet of Things, or IoT, which connects to the cloud everything from home appliances to industrial infrastructure. The cellular industry's next generation of technology, 5G, is being designed to specifically address these needs. Gartner projects[1] that by 2020, there will be over 20 billion IoT devices connected to the Internet representing a $3 billion market. Achieving and sustaining this exponential market growth requires that the wireless technologies underpinning the IoT are secure.

---

[1] http://www.gartner.com/newsroom/id/3165317

Along the way, military and public safety communities have begun embracing commercial wireless technologies as components to their mission-critical communications systems. Examples include FirstNet's use of commercial LTE for public safety users, Wireless Priority System (WPS) for national security and emergency response users, and US military use of WiFi and private LTE networks both domestically and overseas. These critical missions all demand more from a security and resilience perspective than traditional personal and commercial use of these technologies. Additionally efforts to share spectrum between legacy military systems and commercial wireless broadband operators adds an additional wrinkle to understanding security. Unlocking the value of shared spectrum and achieving the economies of scale by leveraging commercial infrastructure are only feasible if these heightened security requirements can be achieved without major changes to the underlying technologies.

Security of Wireless Infrastructure

In order to securely and reliably deliver media and services to wireless devices, we must rely on the underlying security of the infrastructure itself. To better explore this topic, we can break things down into systems operating over licensed spectrum, like cell phones, and those operating over unlicensed spectrum, like WiFi.

Cellular systems have the advantage of being centrally managed which helps ensure that security safeguards are implemented. While industry continues to advance and innovate security safeguards, that security may be undermined by the need to continue supporting backward-compatible legacy technologies. Our new 4G-LTE systems are secure, but the 2G networks are vulnerable to a wide range of attacks that can compromise subscribers' security and privacy. Recently-publicized attacks against the SS7 protocol and unlawful use of IMSI catchers – also known as Stingrays – are examples of risks in legacy 2G systems.

Meanwhile as we look forward from 4G to 5G, a range of new technologies are under development that offer the opportunity to close current cybersecurity gaps while potentially opening up new ones in ways we cannot yet anticipate. Examples include software-defined networking, cloud-based radio access networks, and edge computing – all of which are fueling IoT applications.

Unlicensed technologies have their own challenges. WiFi's adoption in the early 2000s was nearly undermined by sweeping security vulnerabilities. While residential WiFi networks are generally now operating with adequate levels of security, public hotspots and paid WiFi in hotels and airplanes remain vulnerable to attacks that have been well known for nearly two decades. Meanwhile many of the shorter-range wireless protocols used in home and building automation systems are proprietary and lack needed rigorous security analyses.

Lastly, emerging shared bands that involve a coordinated mixture of licensed and unlicensed access will have a blended set of security requirements and security threats. The spectrum sensors and coordination databases represent new attack surfaces and if exploited could disrupt spectrum availability and compromise the privacy of sensitive incumbent activity. In the 3.5 GHz band, rigorous security protections have been developed, but the threat and risk varies from band to band depending on the criticality and sensitivity of incumbent activity.

Security of Wireless Ecosystems

Riding on top of this wireless infrastructure is a complex, interlinked ecosystems of device manufacturers, software and app developers, cloud infrastructure providers, and platforms for media and services. Key cyber threats include exploiting thousands of devices to use them as part of massive Internet attacks, such as the Mirai botnet attack against the Dyn Internet infrastructure company in October 2016; mobile and IoT ransomware, such as the Android ransomware that affected LG smart TVs in January; privacy compromising attacks that steal financial or other personal data, such as the growth of robocalls and SMS phishing attacks; or cyber attacks against safety-critical systems that could lead to loss of life or property, such as the Jeep telematics hack demonstrated in 2015.

The biggest challenge in securing these ecosystems is their complexity and heterogeneity. Over the past decade, this rich tapestry of companies has fueled unprecedented levels of mobile technology innovation, but the consequence is that no one entity controls enough of the ecosystem to unilaterally guarantee the needed security. Another side effect is that regulatory authority is distributed across the Department of Homeland Security, Federal Communications Commission, Federal Trade Commission, and various other sector-specific regulators. Without a single "belly button", top-down approaches to achieving objective levels of security are infeasible.

Consequently it is imperative that we develop mechanisms to foster continued collaboration. In the policy and regulatory arena, the NIST Cybersecurity Framework and the Cybersecurity Information Sharing Act (CISA) are both examples of activities that achieved broad support from both government and industry. Similarly, cyber workforce initiatives from CyberCorps to the National Initiative for Cybersecurity Education (NICE) have had a transformative effect on understanding what skills are needed for these 21st century jobs and incentivizing our nation's education system to implement the needed education and training programs.

Conclusions

Looking forward, I encourage this subcommittee to consider the following.

First, it is imperative that the federal government continue to act as a convener, bringing together this complex cast of characters and help set priorities for cyber defense based on its unique knowledge of the threat. Industry needs consensus issues that they can solve based on a shared understanding of threats to our critical networks and privacy of our citizens.

Second, IoT and 5G wireless represent major shifts in the nature of telecommunications and the Internet. Both industry and the federal government need to significantly increase research funding in these areas so we can work to build security in from the start as these standards are being defined, rather than through after-the-fact solutions applied with duct tape and bubble gum. As an example, last year the National Science Foundation worked with Intel Labs to jointly fund a grant program in IoT security with a total budget of $6M. While this is an excellent example of co-investment, orders of magnitude more resources need to be brought to bear if we hope to get out in front of this problem.

Third, despite many great programs to help bolster the cyber workforce, the nation currently has over a million total jobs in cybersecurity, of which 31% are currently vacant[2]. In the area of cybersecurity for wireless and telecommunications systems the gap is even wider – most universities are shifting curriculum away from large-scale telecom infrastructure toward how to write an app. As a result the number of graduating students with the needed mixture of skills as a ratio of the need is declining. Programs are needed to incentivize universities to build programs to support cybersecurity for telecommunications, and more broadly critical infrastructure.

Thank you for the opportunity to address the subcommittee today and I look forward to questions.

---

[2] http://cyberseek.org/heatmap.html

Mrs. BLACKBURN. The gentleman yields back and we thank you. Ms. Todt, you are recognized for 5 minutes.

STATEMENT OF KIERSTEN E. TODT

Ms. TODT. Good morning, Chairman Blackburn and Ranking Member Doyle and members of the subcommittee. Thank you for the opportunity to present my testimony on the promotion of security in wireless technology. I am currently the managing partner of Liberty Group Ventures and a resident scholar in Washington, DC, at the University of Pittsburgh Institute for Cyber Law Policy and Security.

I also serve on the Federal Advisory Board of Lookout, Incorporated, and most recently served from March 2016 to March 2017 as the executive director of the presidential Commission on Enhancing National Cybersecurity. This Commission was bipartisan independent and was charged with developing actionable recommendations for growing and securing the digital economy as well as for creating a road map for the incoming administration.

I appreciate this subcommittee's awareness of the need to focus on the security of wireless and mobile technology. In a world where first-to-market overrides secure-to-market and every enterprise is seeking to make operations move more quickly and be more convenient, addressing the security of these innovations is critical and absolutely necessary. In response to the questions posed by this hearing, my testimony will primarily focus on mobile security and addressing the growing threat around interdependencies in IoT.

Mobile devices are an attack vector that cannot be ignored and they are increasingly targeted for access to sensitive information or financial gain, as we have heard thoughtfully from our other panelists. But mobility should not be at odds with security and the reality is that cloud and mobile adoption in the enterprise is just beginning.

Mobile devices are a part of every supply chain in your home and in your office, and mobile devices have become much more than communications devices. They are the access point to our work and our personal lives. Additionally, with the rise of two-factor authentication—an important step in ensuring security, but not the ultimate solution—the smart phone has become even more important than the password.

A compromised device could hand over to an attacker an authentication code and thus access to an individual's most personal information as well as any work related sensitive information. All mobile products have latent security vulnerabilities that could be exploited by bad actors and many users ignore security policies and download apps from unofficial sources.

According to a recent Ponemon study, 67 percent of the Global 2000 reported that a data breach occurred as a result of employees using mobile devices to access the company's sensitive and confidential information. Last summer, Lookout and Citizen Lab detected the Pegasus spyware. Pegasus took advantage of three zero-day vulnerabilities in the iOS devices to take complete control of a device.

The attack was capable of getting messages, calls, emails, logs, et cetera from apps including Facetime, Facebook, WhatsApp,

Viber, Skype, Gmail and others. This threat represents the first time anyone has seen a remote jailbreak of an Apple device in the wild and shows us that highly resourced actors see the mobile platform as a fertile platform for gathering information.

Historically, Government agencies have been restrictive about the use of mobile devices in the workplace. Perhaps because agencies now recognize that mobility is happening with or without their permission, we are beginning to see a shift towards prioritizing mobility initiatives in the Federal Government. The bottom line is that smart phones are essentially a super computer, as my colleague Mr. Wright noted, and today most have absolutely no security software on them. Mandates or policies stipulating that mobile devices must have an agent on the device that does predictive analytics should be considered.

I would like to take this opportunity to commend John Ramsey the CISO of the U.S. House of Representatives for his focus and recent action on mobile security. This example is one where Congress is ahead of the executive branch in implementing a cybersecurity best practice, and I encourage this committee, perhaps in collaboration with the House Homeland Security Committee, to hold a hearing on and to examine how Federal agencies can do a better job to defend against mobile security risks and to take a page from the U.S. House of Representatives.

Our interconnections and interdependencies are becoming more complex and now extend well beyond critical infrastructure. These interconnections reduce the importance of the critical infrastructure label because by association all dependencies may be critical as we saw with the Dyn/Mirai attack last fall. The proliferation of IoT devices is a growing challenge, and for the purpose of this hearing I offer the automobile as an example of interconnected devices.

A Tesla is really a giant phone and battery on wheels. The base technology for connected cars originates from the smart phone revolution. And IoT and all of the technology that goes into connected cars, for example, is based on open source code that is genetically related to smart phones.

We need to recognize that neither the Government nor the private sector can capably protect systems and networks without close and extensive cooperation. The mobile environment only adds to the challenge and urgency to develop an approach that emphasizes pre-event collaboration, which I describe in my written testimony, to more effectively manage our collective cybersecurity risk.

As Representative Eshoo noted, Government does instant response well, but we need to be doing more to focus on prevention and collaboration before an event actually occurs. Information sharing is a byproduct of trust that develops through that type of collaboration. We now recognize mobile security as one of the greatest risks affecting all enterprises and we therefore need to treat mobile devices as an endpoint priority equal to, if not more important than, traditional endpoints such as desktops and laptops.

Thank you for the opportunity to testify in front of you today. I look forward to answering your questions.

[The prepared statement of Ms. Todt follows:]

Prepared Testimony of
Kiersten E. Todt

Before the
House Committee on Energy and
Commerce, Subcommittee on
Communications and Technology

Room 2322 Rayburn House Office Building
10AM
Tuesday, June 13, 2017

Liberty Group Ventures, LLC   3033 Wilson Boulevard, Suite 700, Arlington, VA 22201
www.libertygroupventures.com   703.989.5385

I. Introduction

Good afternoon Chairman Blackburn and Ranking Member Doyle. Thank you for the opportunity to present my testimony on the promotion of security in wireless technology. I am currently the Managing Partner of Liberty Group Ventures and a Resident Scholar in Washington, DC at the University of Pittsburgh Institute for Cyber Law, Policy, and Security. I also serve on the Federal Advisory Board of Lookout, Inc. I most recently served, from March 2016 to March 2017, as the Executive Director of the Presidential Commission on Enhancing National Cybersecurity. This independent, bipartisan Commission was tasked by then-President Obama to assess the state of our nation's cybersecurity; this group of twelve Commissioners, four of whom were recommended by leaders of both parties in the Senate and the House of Representatives, was charged with developing actionable recommendations for growing and securing the digital economy. The Commission completed its report on December 1, 2016 and the Chair of the Commission and I presented the key recommendations to then-President Obama. The report includes six imperatives, 16 recommendations, and 53 action items.

I appreciate this Subcommittee's awareness of the need to focus on the security of wireless and mobile technology. In a world where "first to market" overrides "secure to market" and every enterprise – industry, government, and/or individual – is seeking to make operations move more quickly and be more convenient, addressing the security of these innovations is critical and absolutely necessary. In response to the questions posed by this hearing, my testimony will primarily focus on mobile security and address the growing threat environment around interdependencies and the Internet of Things, which I will refer to as IoT.

II. Mobile Security

In this age of data breaches, mobile devices, which are highly portable, constantly connected to various networks, and are being used to access cloud services across personal and enterprise computing, are an attack vector that cannot be ignored. Mobile devices are increasingly targeted for access to sensitive information or financial gain. Mobility should not be at odds with security. As an individual, you should have the freedom to communicate, shop, bank, etc. without worry. And at work, IT/security professionals should be able to secure the sensitive data accessible on their employees' mobile devices, yet still enable business to run as usual.

The growing adoption of mobile in the enterprise has allowed for increased flexibility and productivity. However, due to this shift, mobile devices have rapidly become ground zero for a wide spectrum of risks that includes malicious targeted attacks to devices and network connections, a range of malware families, non-compliant apps that leak data, and vulnerabilities in device operating systems or apps.

The reality is that cloud and mobile adoption in the enterprise is just beginning. Analysts have predicted that mobility-related initiatives will grow from 25 percent of IT budgets to

40 percent in the next 3 years. Therefore, now is the time to implement mobile security. Mobile devices are part of every supply chain – in your home and in your office. We need to treat mobile devices as an endpoint priority equal to, if not more important than, traditional endpoints, such as desktops and laptops.

Mobile devices have become much more than communication devices. They are the access point to our work and personal lives. Today, many individuals bank and make purchases from their devices; they collaborate on sensitive work documents, and they monitor their personal health data. I recently had bloodwork done and was told the only way I could access the results was by downloading an app onto my smartphone. Additionally, with the rise of two-factor-authentication -- an important step in ensuring the security of your accounts, but not the ultimate solution -- the smartphone has become even more important than the password. A compromised device could hand over to an attacker an authentication code -- and thus access to an individual's most personal information, as well as any work-related sensitive information.

Apple has done an excellent job building products with security in mind. They also take tremendous care to ensure that malicious apps do not end up in the App Store. However, when it comes to security, particularly for enterprises or government agencies, it's advisable to exercise a defense-in-depth strategy. All products have latent security vulnerabilities that could be exploited by bad actors. Many users ignore security policies and download apps from unofficial sources. Users can also be tricked into compromising the integrity of their device by installing a malicious profile when connecting to public WiFi networks. Otherwise benign apps can have behaviors (such as accessing data and/or sending it to unknown servers) that violate a company or organization's security policies. To mitigate these risks, an enterprise should have many layers of security protecting the sensitive data that matters most.

Currently, it takes enormous effort to reverse engineer and remediate a cyberattack and only minimal effort for attackers to modify their code and infrastructure to successfully evade detection. As we are often reminded, defense has to be right always – an attacker only has to be right once. An industry over-reliance on signatures and behavioral analysis detection models has much to do with the problem. Signatures can't scale with the pace of malicious software development and they routinely miss advanced attacks. Behavioral analysis models tend to produce more false positives, creating excessive noise that can cause organizations to lose or overlook important signals surfaced by the detection model.

There are currently more than two billion mobile devices worldwide, with more than 4 million apps in app stores being constantly updated, and thousands of device types and OS versions generating hundreds of billions of data points. Effective security for the mobile world analyzes potential mobile threats not in the context of a single server, a single device, or a single application, but in the context of global mobile devices and code.

Some enterprises wonder why they haven't heard of an enterprise data breach resulting from an attack on mobile devices. It's not that the threats aren't there, it's that most organizations don't have visibility into them. According to a recent Ponemon study, 67% of the Global 2000 reported that a data breach occurred as a result of employees using mobile devices to access the company's sensitive and confidential information. In the userbase of Lookout, a leading mobile security company, over the course of six months, they found that on average, 47 out of 1000 Android enterprise devices encountered an app-based threat, including spyware, data exfiltrating trojans, and root enablers that compromise the integrity of the device.

Last summer, Lookout and Citizen Lab detected the Pegasus spyware. Pegasus is a sophisticated form of spyware that was being used against a political activist in the UAE, and possibly other targeted individuals around the world. Pegasus took advantage of three iOS zero day vulnerabilities to take complete control of a device. The attack was capable of getting messages, calls, emails, logs, etc. from apps including Facetime, Facebook, Line, Mail.Ru, KakaoTalk, Calendar, WeChat, SS, Tango, WhatsApp, Viber, Skype, Gmail, and more. This threat represents the first time anyone has seen a remote jailbreak of an Apple device in the wild and shows us that highly resourced actors see the mobile platform as a fertile target for gathering information about targets, particularly high risk groups like activists, and regularly exploit the mobile environment for this purpose.

Mobile Security and the Federal Government

Historically, government agencies have been quite restrictive about the use of mobile devices in the workplace. However, in a survey conducted by Lookout, the government worker finds ways around the rules. In this survey of government workers, 40 percent of employees at agencies with rules prohibiting personal smartphone use at work say the rules have little to no impact on their behavior.

Perhaps because agencies have recognized that mobility is happening with or without their permission, we are beginning to see a shift towards prioritizing mobility initiatives in the federal government. A year ago, mobile wasn't on the top 10 priorities for DHS, now it's in the top 3. We also know that DISA is working on making it possible for employees to access Google Play and the Apple App Store on their mobile devices. As agencies recognize the benefits of mobility and embrace it, they must build in proper security from the beginning.

In general, all government agencies should recognize the risk of spyware, other data exfiltrating trojans, network attacks, operating system and app vulnerabilities, and apps that are otherwise benign but may leak sensitive data. The bottom line is that smartphones are essentially a supercomputer — and today, most have absolutely no security software on them.

The federal government should establish mobile as a core pillar of the security infrastructure. For example, it may be worth considering how mobile could be integrated into the DHS reauthorization bill, which was released last week. Mandates or policies

stipulating that mobile devices must have an agent on the device that does predictive analytics, could make a difference in how government views mobile security. Additionally, as is the case across all enterprises, public and private, senior leadership needs to be educated on mobile security to appreciate that while they may have deployed mobile tools, they haven't deployed mobile security. I would like to take this opportunity to commend John Ramsey, the CISO of the U.S. House of Representatives for recently purchasing 8000 licenses for mobile security technology (from Lookout), which he is in the process of deploying. This example is one where Congress is ahead of the Executive branch in implementing a cybersecurity best practice; I encourage this Committee, perhaps in collaboration with the House Homeland Security Committee, to hold a hearing on and to examine how federal agencies can do a better job to defend against mobile security risks.

Federal agencies must also work to stay ahead of the unintentional mobile security threats of human behavior. This issue is, of course, one that cuts across all elements of cybersecurity. The human is the greatest security threat – and a cyber naïve human is an even greater threat. Today, federal agencies have no insight into the devices and applications accessing their data. So, they have no way to get ahead of potential security issues -- whether they come from malicious actors or unassuming employees. Most agencies today do have policies with regard to the use of mobile devices, however, most will also tell you that they aren't effective because they have no way to enforce them.

The Commission on Enhancing National Cybersecurity highlighted the mobile work environment as the environment of today and the future. Many government agencies are not paying sufficient attention to the mobile threat environment, even as we continue to introduce new devices, systems and platforms that introduce a proliferation of interdependencies into networks and thus new vulnerabilities. As the report states, the concept of the classic security perimeter is largely obsolete. Additionally, the government needs to secure all Department and Agency IT assets, including IoT and other network-connected devices, such as smartphones. With mobile access to sensitive data on the rise and digital data becoming increasingly blurred between physical and cyber assets, strong government-industry collaboration that prioritizes the new frontiers of cyber attacks is imperative to our nation's cybersecurity.

III.   The Growing Threat Environment

As we appreciate the growing threat event, and for the purposes of this hearing, the challenges presented by wireless and mobile security, we appreciate that the increase in interdependencies, across critical infrastructure and non-critical infrastructure, caused by the proliferation of IoT devices is a growing challenge. There are a broad set of recommendations and actions that can be taken to address this threat – depending on which aspect of the challenge one is examining.

Our interconnections and interdependencies are becoming more complex and now extend well beyond critical infrastructure (CI). These interconnections reduce the importance of the CI label because, by association, all dependencies may be critical – as we saw with

the Dyn/Mirai attack last fall. As these linkages grow, so does the need to consider their associated risks. This convergence, combined with increased cybersecurity awareness, creates a unique opportunity to change our current approach to protect the digital economy.

We need to recognize that neither the government nor the private sector can capably protect systems and networks without close and extensive cooperation. Critical infrastructure owners and operators deserve clearer guidance and a set of common understandings on how government responsibilities, capabilities, and authorities can lead to better collaboration and joint efforts in protecting cyberspace.

Today, it is widely assumed and expected that the private sector is responsible for defending itself in cyberspace regardless of the enemy, scale of attack, or the type of capabilities needed to protect against the attack. That makes cyberspace the only domain where we asked companies to defend themselves. This assumption is problematic. The government is – and should remain – the only organization with the responsibility and, in most cases, the capacity to effectively respond to large-scale malicious or harmful activity in cyberspace caused by nation-states – but, with the assistance of an in coordination with the private sector. Our current structure does not set up this type of collaboration.

One initial step that needs to be taken to develop this type of collaboration is the development of an entity, similar to the President's Intelligence Advisory Board, which convenes senior leaders from government and industry to address cybersecurity issues. This entity would focus on pre-event planning. Government does incident response well. But, government does not effectively work and collaborate with industry, routinely, before events occur. Taking a page out of the Pentagon playbook, government and industry should train and exercise together on a regular basis. We continue to develop several initiatives that focus on information sharing – a term that is so overused it has lost its meaning. But, information sharing is not a destination – information sharing is a byproduct of relationships and trust that is built between and among entities. If we are going to truly secure the digital economy and the increased innovations around wireless and mobile technologies, industry and government must have a vehicle for collaboration, which creates value for both. Through this process, government and industry should address cybersecurity through a risk management approach – to ensure an enterprise's approach to cybersecurity takes into full account prioritized assets, resources, and risk appetite.

IV. Conclusion

Companies, large and small, as well as government agencies and other organizations, now have more tools at their disposal to assess and take action to better understand and respond to cyber risks. Once organizations are enabled to better manage those risks, they can make informed decisions about how to apply scarce resources to yield the greatest value. We now recognize mobile security as one of the greatest risks affecting all

enterprises. And, we therefore need to treat mobile devices as an endpoint priority equal to, if not more important than, traditional endpoints, such as desktops and laptops.

America prides itself on fostering the individual entrepreneur, the independent and creative spirit, and the competitor who stands above all others. When it comes to tackling the diverse and broad array of cybersecurity challenges, we need those qualities —but we need joint efforts, collaboration, and cooperation even more. Government and industry each have different strengths and limitations in their cybersecurity capabilities. Mechanisms that clearly define public-private collaboration, joint planning, and coordinated response before, during, and after an event are critical and must be effectively developed. We must have complete awareness of how technologies, especially mobile, are being used and deployed in order to secure those technologies most effectively.

No technology comes without societal consequences. The challenge is to ensure that the positive impacts far outweigh the negative ones and that the necessary trade-offs are managed judiciously. In doing so, we can and must manage and significantly lower cybersecurity risks, while protecting privacy and civil liberties. We must also put in place forward-thinking, coherent policies, developed in a transparent process that enable our institutions and our individuals to innovate and take advantage of the opportunities created by new technology — specifically, for the purposes of this hearing, wireless and mobile technologies.

Thank you for the opportunity to testify in front of you today. I look forward to answering your questions.

Mrs. BLACKBURN. Thank you so much. That was wonderful testimony, zipping right through it. And so we will begin with questions and I will yield myself 5 minutes and begin the questions.

Mr. Wright, I am going to start right there with you. We know and you all have referenced some of the public-private partnership, the Government-industry partnerships that have moved forward and attempted to look at best practices in the mobile cyberspace. NIST, we have mentioned that a couple of times their framework and CTIA Cyber Working Group.

So is standard setting enough, is best practices enough, or do we still need to have a statutorial legislative solution?

Mr. WRIGHT. I think it might be a little early to tell. Right now following some of the NIST and cybersecurity framework guidelines I think is working. I think there are a lot of private sector that are currently adopting part of the executive order. It is going to get more of the Government using the NIST Cybersecurity Framework, but there is a lot of other cooperation going on between public and private sector as well.

I think if WannaCry had happened 2 years ago, it would have been a much different story. Today, this time you had Government and the private sector coming together immediately within hours of the outbreak starting, sharing information, sharing indicators of compromise, and you ended up getting sort of a much, much better result.

At Symantec, I know we take our Government and our private-sector relationships very seriously, most oftentimes focused on law enforcement. But that sort of private-sector industry and Government partnering, I think, really is the key to this. There is no government around that is going to be able to fight this problem alone and there certainly is no private company that is going to be able to fight this alone.

Mrs. BLACKBURN. OK. Anyone else want to add something? Ms. Todt?

Ms. TODT. If I may. So I had the privilege of working with NIST on the development of the Cybersecurity Framework, and one of the reasons why it continues to be so successful is it was developed by industry for industry, so then there is an approach that industry is then allowed to take to understand how to manage its risks.

And I think one of the strong points to the executive order that President Trump released was the focus on risk management, and I think when you are looking for industry and Government to come together having that focus on risk management from a collaboration perspective helps to develop those standards.

What we concluded in the Commission report was that private and public sector they should work together. When they don't work together we should create incentives and when those incentives don't work then we should interfere with regulation and other types of official standards.

Mrs. BLACKBURN. OK, anyone else?

Dr. Clancy, let me ask you. You talked a little bit about the Internet of Things and the connected devices. And of course we have a forum going on today, a showcase dealing with some of that. I want you to expand a little bit on the challenges of securing the IoT devices, especially the wearable technologies, and what would be some of the consequences of our failing to adequately secure IoT devices if you have 20 billion such devices connected to the internet in a few years, and what do you see that framework, those challenges?

Dr. CLANCY. Well, I think that IoT represents a breadth of different products and technologies. You have your internet-connected——

Mrs. BLACKBURN. Right, let's focus on the wearable technologies.

Dr. CLANCY. OK. So with respect to wearable, I think some of the chief concerns are privacy of individual users. And we want to make sure that data that is collected from those devices and ingested into the cloud and used as part of whether it is some health app or some other service to consumers that that data remains private and isn't used to compromise the privacy that use that information.

I think some of the challenges we have are that much of the devices are manufactured overseas. We have supply chain challenges and code quality challenges with the software that is in those devices and that results in devices that we don't know if are robust or not. Many times they connect through unlicensed WiFi devices and there is no strong credentials or authentication that can be used to provide real governance over those devices. There is no way to push out software updates, for example, in a deterministic way if there are vulnerabilities that are discovered.

So I think those are some of the challenges that we face and particularly in the wearable space of IoT.

Mrs. BLACKBURN. Thank you. Before I yield back my time I will, my colleagues across the aisle have mentioned Russia a couple of times. And I would just like to highlight that we have in times past tried to raise Russia and our concerns there is an issue and indeed with items manufactured offshore, I think Huawei. We did a hearing on cyber and Huawei and concerns with Russia and then even in the 2012 Presidential Mr. Romney raised Russia as a concern.

I would also highlight with my colleagues we have privacy and data security legislation we would love to move forward on. We look forward to having them join us in working on these issues. And with that I yield back my time and recognize the gentleman from Pennsylvania for 5 minutes for questions.

Mr. DOYLE. Thank you, Madam Chair. So as the threats we face continue to evolve and grow it seems that we not only need to step up our basic practices of cyber hygiene and best practices, but we need to look to the future. And the witnesses, all of you in your testimony, refer to the shortfall in the workforce for cybersecurity positions.

I know that DARPA in 2016 had the Cyber Grand Challenge and they challenged researchers to create autonomous systems that could defend against cyber attacks. Actually, a team from Carnegie Mellon won that challenge, a victory that we are proud of in Pittsburgh.

But I am curious. How does the panel see autonomous defensive systems addressing this escalation in threats in our workforce shortfalls? And we can just start at Mr. Wright and go down. Please.

Mr. WRIGHT. Certainly the shortage in qualified cyber personnel is a problem today. It is going to be a problem in the future. I think the more that we can move toward autonomous defenses the better off we are going to be. I don't think the technology is there today, but it is getting better every day. That type of innovation I know is a huge focus for not just for Symantec but for other vendors as well.

Mr. DOYLE. Thank you. Mr. Yoran?

Mr. YORAN. I think that there is great promise and certainly progress being made in autonomous defenses, a lot of work going on in the cyber domain around artificial intelligence. From my perspective, the key to success is to scale the talent that we have asymmetrically. Part of that would be through autonomous defense, part of it would be through other technologies which provide the limited number of network defenders to cover more ground.

Dr. CLANCY. I would agree with that. I think the major opportunity with autonomous defense is to act as a force multiplier for those human analysts who ultimately are making decisions about what defenses to deploy and how to manage them. We are seeing a renaissance of artificial intelligence right now with deep learning and early research. Applying that to cybersecurity looks very, very promising. But that will help make existing analysts and cyber defenders more efficient, but they will always still need to be part of the equation.

Mr. DOYLE. Sure.

Ms. TODT. I would like to just approach it from a little bit of a different perspective in the sense that from the workforce we look at the fact—what we heard on the Commission particularly is that there are two issues. The current workforce that we have isn't trained effectively for the skill sets that are needed and we also need to be bringing in additional individuals into the workforce.

But this needs to happen while automation, AI, big data machine learning, are all being developed and so what we have to understand is that the culture of cybersecurity that is being created covers everything. And arguably, everybody is a part of the cyber workforce, so while developing that workforce we are also being able to invest in the innovation that can contribute to the autonomous defense that you mentioned.

Mr. DOYLE. Thank you. Let me ask the panel this also. You know, as we look to the range of threats by government, industry, institution to individuals, we acknowledge we all have a shared responsibility to defend and protect this infrastructure. So what role do you think ISPs can play in mitigating cyber threats whether it be a botnet, malware, or some other threat, do you think Federal agencies should have more authority to mandate either concrete steps or risk mitigation frameworks to ensure that these companies take sufficient steps to protect these networks if they are not doing it on their own? And for anyone on the panel.

Mr. YORAN. Sounds like a dangerous question. I will take a stab at it. I think that there is an opportunity for service providers to differentiate themselves based on security service levels and we have seen a number of service providers take a very proactive approach to their security programs and offer security services and protective services as part of these packages and using it as a differentiation.

When you get to a point of mandating security, I think you are on a very slippery slope and potentially dangerous scenario where the service providers don't necessarily own the applications. They don't understand the ways the systems are being used and what impact might occur if they choose to block certain types of traffic or not.

So there is merit in further investigating the concept, I just think it should be done very cautiously.

Ms. TODT. And I just would like to add, from the executive order this was one of the key issues that was raised and it was also something that created a lot of initial tension with the Commission to understand whose role, who is responsible for what. As Amit said, I mean this is dangerous territory and there was a lot of discussion and debate.

But what the executive order lays out and I think what industry has said is essentially we need to come together to understand where the responsibilities lie and how to create a road map for moving forward. This is clearly an issue for collaboration between industry and Government.

Mr. DOYLE. Thank you. Thank you, Madam Chair. I yield back.

Mrs. BLACKBURN. The gentleman yields back. Mr. Lance, for 5 minutes.

Mr. LANCE. Thank you. I promise no dangerous questions and you have all answered them very beautifully and very adeptly in my judgment.

Dr. Clancy, you mentioned in your testimony that 5G technologies have the opportunity to close current cybersecurity gaps. Can you please expand on what these cybersecurity gaps are and how the industry 5G innovations can help close the gaps?

Dr. CLANCY. I think that as you look at the shift, the technology shift that has happened as we move from the 3G and 2G core network infrastructure to the 4G core network infrastructure, we have moved away from the old circuit switch technology and into all IP-based cell phone backhaul and backbone.

This is creating a range of new opportunities for new technologies and new services that can be provided through this infrastructure and it also exposes much of the cellular infrastructure to the same sorts of risks that you face on the internet. Before, we had a closed circuit switch network that was isolated from the internet; now the barrier between the internet and the cell phone core infrastructure begins to get blurry because of the structure of the 4G infrastructure.

5G actually blurs the line even further with technologies like edge computing, a cloud-based Radio Access Network technology. However, these are new tools in the toolbox that could be used to construct a better set of layered cyber defenses on behalf of subscribers, but we still haven't yet from a research and standards perspective really figured out how all of that will fit together.

Mr. LANCE. Thank you. Mr. Yoran, as we saw with the attack last year, unsecured Internet of Things devices, can pose a threat to the other areas of the internet ecosystem. With billions of IoT devices expected to come to market in the coming years, it is essential that this vulnerability be addressed. Do you see the NIST Cybersecurity Framework as the best approach to address Internet of Things security?

Mr. YORAN. I think the NIST Cybersecurity Framework is probably the best place to begin the dialogue around Internet of Things security. At the end of the day, we have to take a holistic approach to cybersecurity. We can't look at multiple devices independently, we can't look at wireless networks independently or Internet of Things independently. These things are completely intertwined. Internet of Things most frequently rely on wireless networks for their communications so they have to be looked at.

And I think the most important thing from my perspective that the Cybersecurity Framework pushed toward was taking a risk-based approach, because no use of technology is risk-free so understanding it from a risk perspective is really helpful.

Mr. LANCE. Would anyone else on the panel like to comment?

Ms. TODT. Just a quick comment. That is one of the issues that was brought up also in the executive order and from the Commission which is to bring together, as Amit said, bringing together industry and Government based off of the platform. So I think there is motion already in place at NIST to move forward with this to be able to create a set of standards that industry creates for itself.

Mr. LANCE. I couldn't agree with that more in that industry is often ahead of us in Government and we want to work in a cooperative way. But my belief, based upon the last 20 years, is that we are innovative because of the way we have approached this and certainly we want the United States to continue to be the innovative center of the world regarding these matters.

I represent a district that is very heavily involved in technology and in the internet and we want that to continue. We don't want to lose leadership to some other place around the globe. Thank you, Chair, and I yield back a minute.

Mrs. BLACKBURN. And we will take it. And Mr. McNerney, 5 minutes.

Mr. MCNERNEY. I thank the chairwoman. Ms. Todt, in your written testimony you talked about the world where first to market overrides secure to market. Would you agree that we are currently faced with a market failure since those who buy and sell insecure devices now have to bear the full cost of those devices?

Ms. TODT. So I think you have asked a question that is really at the crux of the IoT debate, because as long as we are pushing out innovation without any security guidelines or boundaries we are in this second phase.

A colleague of Mr. Wright's at Symantec was part of the NSTAC report who talked about this first 18-month window that we have passed on the proliferation of IoT devices. And where we are now is that we heard from, in one of our Commission hearings, the CIO of Intel who said we want regulations and standards around IoT devices because we can't possibly compete in this realm where you have small businesses pushing out the innovation.

So we have to think thoughtfully about incentives, penalties, and being able to truly develop secure by design, which is unfortunately becoming one of those terms that is losing its meaning because it is such a common term. But the idea of building security in and having to build software and hardware to certain standards around security has to be a priority right now with, as we have heard, all of the statistics the proliferation of IoT devices that is only going to increase.

Mr. MCNERNEY. Well, you sort of answered my follow-up question already which was I proposed legislation that would require cybersecurity standards to be developed for the devices and for the devices to be certified to meet those standards. Would that help decrease the threat?

Ms. TODT. So I think it actually connects back to an earlier question which is how do we build out the IoT standards? And I would offer that where we have seen such success with the NIST Framework is the fact that industry and Government have worked together and so really looking at that collaboration first and foremost and then being able to inform any legislation.

I think the sequence of that is important because we learn from what industry has done and we have to come together to then develop the standards that you reference.

Mr. MCNERNEY. OK, thank you. Mr. Wright, Symantec's Internet Security Threat Report points to a growing number of attacks on IoT devices. Would requiring the IoT devices to meet baseline cybersecurity standards help decrease that threat? Is your microphone on?

Mr. WRIGHT. It certainly would be something to look into. I also agree that the NIST Cybersecurity Framework is a good place to begin a lot of those discussions. IoT is a little bit strange. The consumer isn't really playing the role of demanding secure products at this point. Some of that could be around awareness. Thirty six percent of the devices that are being manufactured and pushed out there right now have a default password of ADMIN. Some of these are very simple fixes. I think when the consumers are armed and aware of the dangers they have a better chance of driving some of those markets.

Mr. MCNERNEY. Well, although the WannaCry ransomware attack was not the result of insecure IoT devices, I am curious about what lessons we can apply from the attack to IoT device security. How susceptible are IoT devices to ransomware attacks?

Mr. WRIGHT. So we have seen some preliminary more like research around IoT. We did a research project where a smart TV was hacked in ransomware. Like I said earlier in my testimony, criminals are looking for ways to monetize these attacks. They are only bound by their imagination and it is a matter of time before they are able to figure out how to monetize ransomware attacks on devices, on IoT devices.

Mr. MCNERNEY. Well, are there a way that an IoT security or insecurity could result in physical harm?

Mr. WRIGHT. Certainly. IoT devices that are infected can have real-world consequences, absolutely.

Mr. MCNERNEY. And just to explain, how come it is difficult to patch IoT devices?

Mr. WRIGHT. Well, a lot of times these are being shipped out without any possibility of sending out firmware changes. In fact, most of them cannot receive patches or updates.

Mr. MCNERNEY. So could we, in your opinion, rely on voluntary IoT device security from the manufacturers?

Mr. WRIGHT. Well, I do think this needs to be sort of a consensus-driven standard. We need to have private sector involved. We need to have Government involved and sort of find that middle ground, otherwise it is not going to work.

I will point out one thing. The Mirai botnet that we were discussing today, those devices were not manufactured in the U.S. but rather the vast majority of them were manufactured overseas, specifically in China.

Mr. MCNERNEY. OK. Before I yield I just want to say I appreciate Ms. Todt's remark that Government does respond well but needs to do prevention better. Thank you. I yield back.

Mrs. BLACKBURN. Mr. Shimkus, you are recognized for 5 minutes.

Mr. SHIMKUS. Thank you, Madam Chair. And this is an excellent hearing. I do want to thank you all for coming. This is like an arms race. And the reason why I have always enjoyed this committee is that, you know, technology moves faster than we can regulate, hence it is very successful. Well, and that is part of this debate.

I mean, do we do Federal standards and really almost slow up the ability for expansion and new applications or, and so that is why I think most people are talking about consensus base working with the sector, because if we don't we will trip over ourselves and we will slow applications, we will slow development. And that is why I think you see us kind of doing this little kabuki dance between the sides because it is just a very exciting, but there is a lot of dangers out there and people are going to take as was just said, you can't control what the bad actors are going to try to do to get access.

But I also appreciated the comment that for a manufacturer or a provider they can, having secure information is marketable and should be, they could market it as a premium for the services they are providing and I think we have some businesses here that wrap around this. I think the average individual, we understand having a security office in a corporate setting and probably a sub under the security is data security and obviously, you know, this wireless technology and all these things as a subsection.

So when we hire, when you are looking for a computer programmer to go in cyber, in the cyber world, what is a new engineering computer programmer, what are they going to be doing? I am sure there is a plethora of things, but I mean are they just going to be sitting at a screen watching interactions and trying to pick out and identify an attack?

I mean we have all been in, I have been in nuclear, you know, power plants. I have been in data centers. I have been with screens all over the place. Is that what they are doing? Is that what a computer programmer in cybersecurity ends up doing?

Mr. Yoran, do you want to answer that?

Mr. YORAN. I will take a crack at it. In my experience, the best cybersecurity professionals are the ones that just show a tremendous amount of intellectual curiosity in what they are looking at, and sometimes it comes through formal training and discipline and frequently it doesn't. It is usually not the analyst who is sitting behind a screen watching logs go by and trying to pick and choose which one to dig into that is going to make the difference or that is going to scale our industry.

If I could, I think the comment that you made and the Congressman from California are, I won't say two sides of the same coin, but they point to this foundational question of, you know, is there a market failure and what can and should Congress do about it. And from my experience, I think it would be hard to argue that a market, you know, we are not at a point of market failure, everything from, you know, the election to the hack that you see in every newspaper or news distribution point, even real news distribution point on a daily basis.

In order for free markets to work you have to have an educated populous and you have to have a high degree of transparency and I think in the cyber domain we lack that transparency. There is a general lack of appreciation for what the threat environment looks like. There isn't a consistent understanding of what good cybersecurity looks like, what is working in our domain. There is a lack of transparency when breaches occur outside of ones that impact PII.

And so there isn't a common appreciation for what is not working and also I think what is at stake and what is at risk in using various products. So I think that there is a role for Congress to play around helping to raise awareness and create greater transparency.

Mr. SHIMKUS. Let me go to just Dr. Clancy real quick because my time is running out. When we travel, which we as Members get a chance to do, we are visiting troops, many times we are asked to leave our computer at home and we are given a little dinky one to be able to continue to communicate. How are we, how secure is the U.S. wireless system versus places else around the world?

Dr. CLANCY. I would say the United States has the most secure wireless infrastructure in the world. I think the things that lead to insecurity in other countries' networks have to do with deployment and use of old technology, a workforce that is managing those networks that is not aware of the latest threats, and the influence of authoritarian regimes over state-owned telecom infrastructure providers in many of those countries.

Mr. SHIMKUS. Thank you very much. Thank you, Madam Chairman.

Mrs. BLACKBURN. Ms. Matsui, you are recognized for 5 minutes.

Ms. MATSUI. Thank you, Madam Chair, for having this hearing and I thank the witnesses for being here today. Wireless technology and connectedness and of data and information have huge potential to move us forward in a variety of industries.

Ms. Todt, you mentioned in your testimony that you recently had blood work done and were told the only way you could access the results was by downloading an app on your smart phone. I see both potential for good and for danger in this situation. It may be much more convenient for you to receive your test results visually on your phone rather than via snail mail or fax or a phone call. This could result in you acting on that information in a more timely or consistent manner, potentially improving your health.

However, that also means that your data is potentially vulnerable. We saw the risk with the recent malware attacks that brought down hospital systems. Without access to the information that the doctors and nurses relied on to treat their patients they could no longer do so effectively.

Our healthcare system is uniquely at risk of attacks. Most professionals who go into the healthcare field often including administrators don't have a cybersecurity background. We need to work to ensure that our healthcare providers have the technological infrastructure and workforce to manage the complex data that they need to best serve patients.

Last week, the Department of Health and Human Services released its Healthcare Industry Cybersecurity Task Force Report. Among other things, the report recommended executive education about the importance of cybersecurity. Ms. Todt and any of the other witnesses, what recommendations do you have for developing cybersecurity leadership in industries such as health care?

Ms. TODT. Thank you. I am now convinced given what the chairman said that I was one of the 100 million that got my healthcare records breached last year, but that is something else for me to figure out. I think that what you ask is a great question in relation to also the other questions that have been posed around IoT and workforce, because we tend to think of cybersecurity workforce as those with the engineering degrees.

But what we have to understand in the workforce that we are creating is that everybody has to be educated on cybersecurity. This is not an expertise; it crosses every enterprise. And arguably, I would think that human resources professionals, those who are hiring, have to have a baseline level of knowledge. The other issue is that when you are a manager you have to be trained in cybersecurity so that you know what you are doing regardless of whether or not your function is cyber related.

And I think enterprises need to be looking at cybersecurity education the way, as an onboarding process, the way they look at ethics and integrity and basic company protocols and procedures. We have to be incorporating cybersecurity awareness and education from the ground up to create this culture and I think that this is something as we move forward to emphasize.

The other issue that this is more of a technical response but we talk about the education of user awareness. From a technology perspective while we are educating the consumers and the individuals and industries and enterprises, we also need to be thinking about moving security away from the end user from an innovation perspective.

Ms. MATSUI. OK. Thank you very much and let me move on to Dr. Clancy. Dr. Clancy, according to one study, none of America's top-10 computer science programs as ranked by the U.S. News and World Report in 2015 required graduates to take one cybersecurity course. Three of the top 10 programs didn't offer an elective in cybersecurity.

But with the rise of cyber attacks and security breaches in our networks and the shortage of cybersecurity professionals, it is imperative that our students graduate with the course work needed to be able to tackle security issues. Dr. Clancy, how can Congress encourage our colleges and universities to prepare students either through expanding courses, hiring more faculty, or other innovative solutions for careers in cybersecurity?

Dr. CLANCY. So I think the reason you may see that in some of the top-ranked programs is it is the traditional academic culture that cybersecurity is a buzz word and is a fad, and myself and others in academia are working very hard to convince them otherwise that this is a fundamental problem that is going to be with us indefinitely. I think there are a number of programs that are very positively impacting this ecosystem to include NSA's Centers of Academic Excellence program and the CyberCorps Scholarship for Service program.

While the CyberCorps program provides scholarship money for students to pursue careers in Government upon graduation like a cyber ROTC program, the funding helps the university establish a platform that can educate students in cybersecurity who go into many different careers, not just into Federal Government. We saw that directly at Virginia Tech as part of our receipt of a CyberCorps grant. I think more initiatives and further investment in programs like that is a great place to start.

Ms. MATSUI. OK, thank you. And I have run out of time, I yield back.

Mrs. BLACKBURN. Mr. Olson, you are recognized.

Mr. OLSON. I thank the Chair and welcome to all of our witnesses. Mr. Yoran, thank you, sir, for your service to our country in our United States Army, West Point graduate. Heartfelt congratulations as well, because with assist from Temple for the first time in 15 years your Navy beat my Army in football. Bravo Zulu.

Your testimony talks about elastic attack surface that includes a growing number of information technology devices. Being the vice chairman of the Energy Subcommittee, I worry about cyber attacks on our power grid. December 23rd, 2015, 230,000 people in the Ukraine were without power for 1 to 6 hours, a cyber attack likely coming from Comrade Putin in Russia. It was very low tech. They simply remotely flipped some switches.

What kind of advice does your company provide to critical infrastructure companies in our electric grid regarding how to best protect their systems for cyber attack?

Mr. YORAN. Thank you, Congressman. I think that is an ongoing challenge. As early as last night, the US–CERT program issued additional warning and guidance to energy and critical infrastructure companies around the Crash Override piece of malware which is affecting power companies around the world.

From a security perspective there is a great challenge in that industry in that the systems are incapable of being updated or there is tremendous risk in updating those systems which, unlike our mobile phones or desktop PCs, have a life span measured in decades. From a best practices perspective these organizations have historically left those critical networks in the standalone state, but increasingly they are interconnected.

We offer technologies and other companies offer technologies that help monitor these networks on a passive basis, so without introducing additional risk, additional packets, or probing those networks you can see what they are vulnerable to and you can create a series of compensating controls to protect those systems from internet compromise.

Mr. OLSON. Also you brought up artificial intelligence. And as a co-chair of the recently launched Artificial Intelligence Caucus, I believe it is important that we use cybersecurity technology to complement the work of the talented human brains that make this happen.

We know that technology alone won't solve the cybersecurity issues we have, but can you elaborate on how leveraging this technology for the growing AI field will work do you think, cybersecurity in the AI field—or Mr. Wright, Dr. Clancy, Ms. Todt? Somebody want to take that? It is not bomb, not a grenade.

Dr. CLANCY. I am happy to take a stab at that. I think the DARPA Cyber Grand Challenge that we saw last year is an example of a first step in being able to accomplish that. As I mentioned earlier, I think that AI will become initially a tool that helps analysts do their job more effectively and more scalably to deal with the growing threat and larger and larger amounts of data.

There is an AI renaissance that is happening, right. There are fundamental advancements that are happening that are completely changing the world of image processing and search that Google and others are leading. And I think there are many in the cybersecurity community that are hoping that those technologies can be applied to the cyber problem, but that is still an early research area that many people are sort of feverishly working on right now in academia.

Mr. OLSON. Ms. Todt, you look like you are chomping at the bit to comment. Am I reading that wrong?

Ms. TODT. Just in support I think that we need to be investing obviously in innovation. I was on a panel with somebody who used to work at DARPA who essentially talked about the fact that there are functions that really aren't meant for humans and that our ability to automate and make those functions more capable through super-computing will help our systems work more effectively.

Mr. OLSON. One final question for you, Mr. Yoran. We are seeing an explosion of free WiFi hotspots all around the country, whether they are there at the corner coffeehouse, the Starbucks, the airport, the airplanes you mentioned; heck, the Mr. Carwash right down the street from my house. My daughter and wife go there all the time. It has a free hotspot just for the 20 minutes you are there.

Do they offer unique challenges to safeguard? If so, what should be done on the network side as opposed to the user side?

Mr. YORAN. Well, I think the most important thing is to recognize that whether you are going to a public hotspot or you get fooled into connecting to a rogue hotspot or you are connected to a corporate network which is already compromised and frequently is, the most important thing that you can do and that organizations can do is better assess the vulnerability and exposure of their systems and make sure that they are applying the latest patches and they don't fall victim. A vast majority of the attacks that we see come from well-known, well established vulnerabilities to which patches are readily available.

Mr. OLSON. Good luck, Army. I yield back.

Mrs. BLACKBURN. Mrs. Dingell, you are recognized.

Mrs. DINGELL. Thank you, Madam Chair, and thank you for doing this hearing and to all of the witnesses. There are so many questions. Cybersecurity is something that should concern all of us. And as somebody who has been hacked more than anybody would want to be I can tell you it is a pain to have to change your password and switch to two-factor authentication and worry about personal information being compromised.

I think what—and not even what I prepared—what is really worrying me is some of the factoids that you have raised here today. I think one of the issues is training people. Even when you have trained IT people and you go to them and you ask a question—ask John Podesta, myself have done this—"Should I do this?" And they say, "Oh yes," and then it turns out not to be the right thing. I think I got one last night that I have now been burnt so much I was smart enough to wait and talk to somebody today.

And I really worry about, as we start to talk about autonomous vehicles, as an example, if people don't—how are we going to make sure patches that need to occur occur, and when they don't, even when we look at the health care, what happened on the health care situation, there were simple patches available that users aren't using. How do you legislate that? These are real issues.

But for these 5 minutes, which are now down to 3 minutes and 45 seconds, let's talk about mobile phones, which as you said, Mr. Wright, are basically super computers we have in our pockets. Our phones are always by our sides. We store our most intimate and personal details in them. And it is happening now and in the near future people are going to be locked out of their phones and in turn will be locked out of personal, social, financial information. That is a new experience for everyone. We are going to see this high level of hysteria, and we have got to pay attention to it.

So this question is for the entire panel. Ransomware is now available as a service making it incredibly easy for criminals to carry out an attack. What can Government do from a policy perspective to increase barriers to entry and the cost of carrying out ransomware attacks, and do you think the threat of a ransomware attack on a mobile device will only continue to increase if the Government doesn't do something, any of the panel?

Mr. WRIGHT. I can start out here. Starting with your last question I think that mobile ransomware will probably increase no matter what is done. Again the criminals follow the money and right now your handheld computer is where that money or where that data is. When they can figure out how to monetize locking up that phone or encrypting that data on your phone enough to the point where you will pay to get it back, then in that case mostly not get the data back, they will exploit that.

Mr. YORAN. I don't think any of us are comfortable with the state of security on mobile phones, but I think a lot of progress has been made. A lot of lessons have been learned in the—some have not, but a lot of lessons have been learned in the mobile domain from decades of mistakes and accidents in operating systems and in compute platforms from the desktop paradigm.

So I am confident that we will see an increase in ransomware no matter what is done on mobile platforms given how attractive they are as a target, but I think the industry is making progress to make that more and more challenging over time.

Dr. CLANCY. I think that if you look at ransomware it is leveraging the same vulnerabilities that people have used to exploit mobile devices for the last decade. So continued work to make sure patches are deployed and apps are updated is critical to closing the front door, if you will, to ransomware.

I think other areas that are somewhat unique to ransomware have to do with educating users about the importance of backing up their data so if they are a victim of ransomware attack they are able to recover their data. Many cellular providers offer free services to back up your data on your phone to the cloud and consumers need to take advantage of that.

Secondly, I think there is really the forensic and law enforcement side of being able to follow the money and be able to take down the ransomware networks which is increasingly difficult with the rise of bitcoin and other crypto currencies, but that is perhaps a larger question.

Ms. TODT. I think ransomware represents sometimes a little bit of the flavor of the day in that we have these problems that continue to evolve, but the solutions for them are the same when we look at WannaCry which was, you know, essentially not updating with patches that are there. So it is a lot of the cyber hygiene that we have talked about and the regular download.

I think it is also important, you raise an interesting element to this which it is often important to remember that attacks and when data is compromised or manipulated it is not usually because there is some engineering expertise or genius, it is really about opportunism and being able to access and exploit that opportunism. And so that is why education, backing up, all of those very basic actions can really cover about 80 percent of the solution.

Mrs. DINGELL. I had more questions, but I am out of time. Thank you, Madam Chair.

Mrs. BLACKBURN. And we will give the opportunity to submit those questions in writing. Mr. Johnson, you are recognized, 5 minutes.

Mr. JOHNSON. Thank you, Madam Chairman.

Mr. Yoran, in your testimony you note that there is a shortage of skilled labor in the cybersecurity workforce. How acute is that shortage? Has it manifested itself in your company? Do you have a problem hiring those kind of people in your own business?

Mr. YORAN. That is a great question. It is extremely competitive to hire experienced cybersecurity professionals. The compensation is great and as they continue to gain experience, you know, their expectations continue to rise.

Mr. JOHNSON. On the technical or the strategic side, because I mean there is a big difference between people that understand what cybersecurity is and those people that can get down to the ones and zeros and kind of do the technical wherewithal to find out who the bad guys are.

Mr. YORAN. I think there is really a shortage on both fronts, which is why I think the importance of Dr. Clancy's comments around the multidisciplinary approach to cybersecurity. What we found is in addition to compensation there is two other critical aspects to attracting and retaining cybersecurity talent. One is in providing them intellectually stimulating work. It is an exciting field and if you don't give them exciting problems they will go elsewhere to find them. And the other is in creating a culture that is dynamic and one that is enjoyable to be part of.

Mr. JOHNSON. OK. Do you think we have the same level of expertise shortage in finding skilled workforce in Government agencies or departments? Is it worse, the same?

Mr. YORAN. I don't know that I have the data in front of me to comment whether it is worse or the same. I do know that a tremendous amount of expertise in the private sector starts out getting its experience in public service which is costly to the Government in terms of losing that talent, but I think it provides tremendous value to the private sector in terms of the level of maturity and understanding of very sophisticated cyber threats.

Mr. JOHNSON. OK, all right. Thank you.

Dr. Clancy, what a name for a topic like cybersecurity. And if your first name was Tom you would be——

Dr. CLANCY. It actually is.

Mr. JOHNSON. Yes. I would consider changing it if I were you.

Dr. CLANCY. No, no, seriously, my name is Tom Clancy.

Mr. JOHNSON. OK, all right. Will the real Tom Clancy please stand up?

Dr. CLANCY. I go by my middle name Charles. It causes too much confusion.

Mr. JOHNSON. Well, Dr. Clancy, how soon should we expect biometric tools to supplant the traditional pin and password approach to device security?

Dr. CLANCY. So biometrics have offered a tremendous opportunity to fundamentally change how we authenticate people. I think there are still challenges. The joke in the biometrics community is that if I am using a fingerprint as my password I can only change my password nine times before I run out of fingers.

So there are some challenges there. If your fingerprint data is compromised because it is stored in a database then your credential is sort of irrevocably lost and you can't change it like you can change a password.

Mr. JOHNSON. So in that regard then, in that vein do you think biometric tools are going to make us more secure or are we going to happen upon the same kinds of problems that we have now if we file them away?

Dr. CLANCY. I believe that biometrics will be a critical part of multifactor authentication. If combined with a password and a mobile device, right, you can fuse these things together in order to significantly improve the security of a particular authentication to some online service.

Mr. JOHNSON. All right. Secondary question, do you think it is right to think of every connected device as a potential vulnerability and, if so, what freedom or flexibility should network operators have to promote security when device owners fail to do so? And I guess we are sort of getting into the Internet of Things, you know.

Dr. CLANCY. Certainly. So the internet service providers have an increasingly challenging time. Because of the rise of technologies like end-to-end encryption, it is very difficult for internet service providers to tell the difference between a botnet command and control packet or a standard IoT web service traffic just because they don't have the visibility that they would otherwise have.

So I think that that creates problems for them that makes it a challenge for the entire ecosystem, where you need the IoT service providers and the device manufacturers and all of them to come together to come up with a common solution for securing IoT.

Mr. JOHNSON. OK. Ms. Todt, I apologize. I had a question for you but I have run out of time. Madam Chair, I yield back.

Mrs. BLACKBURN. Well, we will also let you submit that question in writing. OK, Ms. Clarke, you are recognized for 5 minutes.

Ms. CLARKE. Well, thank you, Madam Chair. The FCC just announced the newest members of the Communications Security, Reliability and Interoperability Council, a council established to make recommendations about the security, reliability, and resiliency of our communications systems. But as I have reviewed the names of the new members, I am disappointed to see a lack of cybersecurity expertise on the council.

As the author of the Cybersecurity Responsibility Act, my bill makes it clear that the FCC has a role in ensuring our commercial sector has protections in place to secure our communication networks from malicious cyber attacks. So Ms. Todt, what role do you believe the Federal Government, in particular the FCC, has in protecting our Nation's communication networks?

Ms. TODT. Well, I think again we can look to the executive order that was released by President Trump in May which specifically calls out the FCC as having a role in protecting the communications infrastructure and working with the secretary of commerce and the secretary of the Department of Homeland Security to initially look at that botnet mitigation, but then also looking at clean pipes and where that goes. And so clearly, I think the Government, the executive office as well as industry, believes that there is a role that it needs to play.

Ms. CLARKE. So then it would be prudent to have some cybersecurity expertise on this council, wouldn't it?

Ms. TODT. That would appear to be the case, absolutely. I don't know who those individuals are, so I don't know if they have them in any——

Ms. CLARKE. Just generally speaking.

Ms. TODT. But I would say, I mean, this is the issue, the broader issue, is that we have to be bringing cybersecurity expertise into all of these areas and that we have to be looking for that because that knowledge and that expertise has to be informing our policies, because they don't even have to be cybersecurity policies but they have an impact.

Ms. CLARKE. Absolutely, thank you.

Dr. Clancy, as part of Congress' resolution of disapproval that overturned the FCC's privacy protections, Congress also stripped away consumers' data security protections. As I noted before, my bill, the Cybersecurity Responsibility Act, would ask the FCC to take some action, any action to protect our networks. Did Congress' rollback of these data security rules do anything to make America's personal information more secure?

Dr. CLANCY. So I think the rollback of the cybersecurity provisions in the FCC rulemaking from 2018 was, actually happened before Congress acted, right. The FCC removed those provisions and stayed those portions of the regulation, and then ultimately Congress rescinded the entire order which was focused more on the privacy aspects of that rulemaking.

Of course the state of rationale was that it was inconsistent with the Federal Trade Commission's view of privacy and opt-in versus opt-out when it comes to consumer privacy. I don't know that I am in a position to declare whether opt-in or opt-out is a more appropriate way to protect consumer privacy, but I think it represents some of the regulatory challenges we have in asserting that one particular regulator has authority over a very complex ecosystem.

Ms. CLARKE. Or the question was more about security. And just looking at the ecosystem, if you sort of strip those or rollback those security rules, we are trying to figure out whether people's personal information it becomes, did we open up vulnerabilities? Let's put it that way.

Dr. CLANCY. So based on my experience working with the cellular industry and some of the major internet service providers, the big companies are already doing those best practices. The large ISPs, the large wireless carriers are already doing that. Where the gap is is the smaller and more rural internet service providers and the more niche wireless carriers who don't have as much infrastructure or resources themselves to deploy those best practices.

Ms. CLARKE. Yes. So when there is a vulnerability even in the smallest of these providers, doesn't that open up opportunities to get at grander——

Dr. CLANCY. Certainly, it does given the interconnectedness of the different telecom providers. I think what we are seeing in industry is strong collaboration though, with the big guys looking out for the small guys and doing what they can to help quickly remediate through information sharing that was really accelerated by the past——

Ms. CLARKE. Anyone else have any thoughts on that?

Ms. TODT. I think the supply chain is a huge issue and even if you are sharing those practices we have to be looking at baseline level of standards. And I think that you are, oh, it is always going to be the weakest link and we have to do a better job within our sectors of actually informing and helping to share those best practices and lessons learned.

One of the things that we have learned is that small businesses across sector have a lot more in common with each other than the small businesses and the large businesses within their sector and there is a lot of evidence right now around that. And so being able to look at this more thoughtfully and I think it goes again to this issue of collaboration and pre-event planning would be the actions that we need to be taking.

Ms. CLARKE. Very well. Madam Chair, I yield back. Thank you.

Mrs. BLACKBURN. And Mr. Bilirakis, you are recognized for 5 minutes.

Mr. BILIRAKIS. Thank you, Madam Chair. I appreciate it so much. And I appreciate your testimony today.

As more IoT devices enter the market industry has seen a rise in tech support scams, unfortunately. Symantec's 2016 Threat Report found a 200 percent rise in tech support scams in a 2-year period. With these types of threats the best defense is with the end user. Mr. Wright, how can an end user distinguish between a legitimate help desk and a tech support scam and can you describe how Symantec has responded to the increased threat?

Mr. WRIGHT. Yes. So these types of social engineering attacks as you just mentioned the tech support are particularly vexing. They depend on the consumer to somehow be able to intuit or to understand whether or not they are being, whether they are being scammed. There is not a lot of sort of technology that can fix that. A lot of it comes back to raising awareness of the user of what those threats could be, those users being more careful and perhaps having a more keen eye on to pick up signs. But it is a very, very difficult problem when it comes down to the user themselves.

Mr. BILIRAKIS. Yes, thank you. For years people have been told to check for the https identifier in their browser before accessing personal websites such as for banking or health care. Mr. Wright again, your 2016 Threat Report states that relying on the https marking provides a false sense of security. Can you expand upon that?

Mr. WRIGHT. I am sorry?

Mr. BILIRAKIS. Your findings. No, let me say it again. Your 2016 Threat Report states that relying on the https marking provides a false sense of security. Can you expand on that finding?

Mr. WRIGHT. I know that https is more protected, but I am sorry I cannot sort of expand on the Internet Security Threat Report piece there. I am not prepared for that. Anybody on the panel have——

Mr. BILIRAKIS. OK. Can maybe anyone else on the panel? Yes, please.

Dr. CLANCY. So https implies that the session is authenticated and encrypted, but the concern is to whom you are authenticated. There are many scams that can change a letter in the name of the domain name such that you wouldn't notice the difference but could still present a secure credential to you as a user.

So I think https is a first step, and if you don't have that then you definitely need to be concerned. You need to look at the spelling of the domain name to make sure that it is spelled accurately and there aren't strange characters in there, that those are the sorts of things that undermine the security of simply looking for the https.

Mr. BILIRAKIS. Any other suggestions?

OK, thank you very much. Let's see, I still have a little time. Mr. Wright, according to Symantec 2016 Threat Report, the Apple iOS system faced its first widespread threat with the XcodeGhost attack. This malware has infected over 4,000 apps which leaves unsuspecting devices vulnerable. In response to cyber threats success largely depends on speed of response. How has industry responded to threats via apps since it first took hold in 2015 and have efforts met the success?

Mr. WRIGHT. Yes, good question. So apps certainly represent a potential threat vector especially for mobile devices. I would say that Apple has done a pretty good job making sure that malicious apps are not included in their app store. Android is doing a better job at trying to ensure that their apps aren't malicious. So those two providers I think have come a long way. Apple has always been pretty good, but the other provider has come a long way.

In addition, there is some security solutions to this. Not plugging Symantec, but we do produce technology that can scan for apps and look for possible malicious apps or grayware apps which sometimes can leak information. So there is a technology solution, and then also the providers are doing a lot of work in that area as well.

Mr. BILIRAKIS. Anyone else want to add something? I know I only have 15 seconds. OK, very good. Thank you, Madam Chair. It is a very informative hearing. Thanks for calling the hearing. Thank you.

Mrs. BLACKBURN. Thank you. Ms. Eshoo, 5 minutes.

Ms. ESHOO. I thank the chairwoman and I thank all the witnesses. I think you have given very important testimony. First of all, to Mr. Wright, I am very proud to represent Symantec.

Mr. WRIGHT. Thank you.

Ms. ESHOO. I have had a long, long, long-term relationship going back to the days of John and how he really helped build a new Symantec and you keep going and you are a real asset to the country.

And to Mr. Yoran, you get the prize for the best dressed before this subcommittee every time you come. One of the members said, do you think he lost his suitcase? I said, no, he hasn't lost his suitcase. That is his tuxedo for this committee.

There has been a lot of discussion about a lot of things here. The title of the hearing is Cybersecurity Risks to Wireless Networks, but this is an entire ecosystem. And I think we have made real progress in many areas and I think that obviously we are lacking in others. I want to thank Symantec for working with me on the legislation that I mentioned in my brief opening statement.

But I want to go to something else first and then a question to each one of you. Last year the FCC put into place data security rules that apply to wireless carriers as part of its privacy proceeding. And Dr. Clancy, you just gave some kind of, I don't know really what it was, but I am going to find out more, press you for more.

These rules asked ISPs, really, something very simple and that is to take, quote, reasonable measures, reasonable measures to protect consumer data. Now there was the monetization of information and the monetization of attacks that has been brought up by more than one panel member this morning. Do any of you think that the FCC went too far in asking ISPs to act reasonably to protect consumer data?

There is a little bit of, if I might suggest this, politically cross-dressing that is going on here, because the Congress ripped away all privacy protections on the internet and that is on the computer that I have in my purse. That is for everyone in the country. So we are talking about, I think cybersecurity is all about privacy. It brings about privacy.

So maybe a yes or no to each one of you, and if you don't know, then say that. Do you think the FCC went too far in asking for reasonable measures to protect consumer data? I am going to start with——

Mr. WRIGHT. So I will have to say I don't know too much about that——

Ms. ESHOO. OK.

Mr. WRIGHT [continuing]. Specifically, but I will say, you know, it appears to be reasonable to protect user data.

Mr. YORAN. I can't comment specifically to FCC's issue, but reasonable does sound reasonable.

Dr. CLANCY. Indeed. I mean it was a complicated set of circumstances, but——

Ms. ESHOO. What is so complicated about it? What is complicated about it? I have it right here what they put forward. They are really simple things.

Dr. CLANCY. Reasonable is reasonable.

Ms. TODT. I will ditto my colleagues. I mean, reasonable protections are reasonable.

Ms. ESHOO. I think what I would like to do in writing, because I don't have time for it, is to ask each one of you so you can be prepared for it, what is your top line recommendation to the subcommittee relative to cybersecurity in our country? Just one thing, top line, from each one of you. You are all experts and I will look forward to sending that to you and getting your responses. Thank you for what you are doing for the American people. I appreciate it.

Mrs. BLACKBURN. All right. Let's see, Mr. Flores, you are recognized.

Mr. FLORES. Thank you, Madam Chair, and I want to thank the panel for being here today.

Ms. Todt, unlike other types of crimes, when we talk about cybercrime we always seem to focus on the need to protect against the attacks rather than prosecute the bad actors. And can you tell us what the Federal Government is doing to actively work on cybercrime attribution and also what are the limitations of trying to track down our cyber adversaries?

Ms. TODT. So right now I believe the executive order has laid out—I am not as familiar with the criminal angle. I know we worked with the Department of Justice with the Commission on being able to look at malicious actors and where the crime plays a role, and I think one of the key things that a lot of the commissioners talked about is you have to have penalties for those bad actors. But I apologize, I can't talk extensively, but I am happy to get back to you with an answer in writing.

Mr. FLORES. OK, yes. If you could do that, that would be great.

Dr. Clancy, in your testimony today and from testimony across the panel it sounds like we have got a skills gap when it comes to protecting ourselves from cybercrime. And of course in order to fill the pipeline we are going to have to be able to get our educational institutions to produce the people resources to be able to do with this.

I represent three world-class universities back in my district, Texas A&M University, Baylor University, and the University of Texas. What could the Federal Government be doing to help ensure that pipeline is filled with quality skilled individuals?

Dr. CLANCY. I think that most of the efforts to date have focused on the tail end of the pipeline.

Mr. FLORES. Right.

Dr. CLANCY. Getting students out of college and into jobs, I think the pipeline starts much earlier than that.

Mr. FLORES. Exactly.

Dr. CLANCY. When students are coming into college they need to want to major in cybersecurity and more broadly in STEM fields, so I think additional initiatives that are focused on the K–12 outreach and engagement to bring cybersecurity down to the middle school level or even sooner, just basic digital hygiene at the elementary school level would be a great starting point and build up from there. If you want to build a pipeline you need to start at the beginning.

Mr. FLORES. OK. Now Mr. Yoran, you and I both have business backgrounds and I mean you hire a lot of these types of individuals. What would your key recommendations be?

Mr. YORAN. I think it is important for employers to look for the intellectual curiosity around cyber. And as Dr. Clancy said earlier, you know, I think you have to start at an earlier age and part of it may be through cyber hygiene. I know I could talk to my kids about cyber hygiene and they still don't apply their patches, so I think we have to find things that are more interesting, more intriguing ways of creating excitement and creativity around cybersecurity education.

Mr. FLORES. OK, thank you.

Dr. Clancy, you mentioned the need for the Federal Government to continue to act as a convener and to set priorities based on its unique knowledge of cyber threats, but for national security reasons the Government doesn't always share the full extent of its knowledge of those threats. How significant is this limitation and how can Congress be helpful in encouraging more transparent threat intelligence sharing?

Dr. CLANCY. So I think from a convening perspective, groups like the FCC CSRIC organization is a great way for the Government, for the Federal Communications Commission, to sort of set priorities and identify areas of concern and work collaboratively with industry to identify solutions. I think that that goes to a certain extent hand in hand with the challenges of cyber information sharing.

You have the national security agencies who are generating detailed information on cyber threat, but that is due to the sources and methods involved. It is held at a classified level and can't be shared and that creates a barrier to sharing. The thought is that if we have sufficiently large cyber threat brokerage houses sort of emerging that there can be enough data that the Federal Government could anonymously share data that would obscure sources and methods with those brokerages and it wouldn't be attributable to specific sensitive aspects of how that data was arrived at.

Now we are not there yet, but I think there is some hope that that may be a solution moving forward long term.

Mr. FLORES. OK, thank you. If any of you have any supplemental comments on any of these questions and you could submit those, that would be great. Thank you, and I yield back the balance of my time.

Mrs. BLACKBURN. Mr. Rush, you are recognized for 5 minutes.

Mr. RUSH. I want to thank you, Madam Chair, and I want to commend you for holding this hearing.

Dr. Clancy, Tom, you are concerned that the Internet of Things, the IoT, where everything from home appliance to industrial infrastructure devices connected to the internet is not secure enough to withstand a cyber attack. What is the biggest challenge you see in securing this complex mobile ecosystem?

Dr. CLANCY. Well, I think that just the breadth, as you stated, is part of the challenge. The threats to an internet-connected home appliance are very different than the threats to an internet-connected nuclear reactor and the technologies involved are very different.

So at one end of the spectrum in the consumer technology space we have the key challenge, I think, is supply chain and inexpensive goods, inexpensive IoT devices coming from overseas that were not designed with security as part of the fundamental component. I think at the other end of the spectrum you have industrial infrastructure, industrial control systems. There the challenge is more that the desire to gain efficiencies from aging infrastructure and be able to support more users with the same power grid and more peak demand requires us to use artificial intelligence to orchestrate much of our infrastructure which necessitates connecting that infrastructure to the cloud in order to do the needed big data processing on the data.

So you end up drawing this sort of series of events that necessitates for business reasons connecting this industrial infrastructure to the cloud, which then fundamentally exposes it to risks it had never faced before. And that is a whole separate set of challenges that requires the key components of that industry to figure out how to work together to solve those challenges.

Mr. RUSH. Are you concerned that the Federal Government is inadequate and then presently is organized that we are, are we prepared to deal with this broad threat, a cybersecurity threat? I mean we have different centers of responsibility or authority and power located in many different places from Homeland Security to the FCC. Are we prepared in a streamlined way to respond to a cyber attack using these IoTs?

Dr. CLANCY. I think we are never going to be as prepared as we would like to be, but I think our level of preparedness is steadily increasing. I think the NIST Cybersecurity Framework that many have referenced throughout this hearing is a great example of a tool that we can use to develop a common understanding of how to respond to these threats and we need more things like that to help improve our ability to respond.

Mr. RUSH. I want to thank you. I want to move to Mr. Wright. Mr. Wright, how vulnerable is the U.S. power grid to a similar power grid attack that Ukraine suffered last year?

Mr. WRIGHT. Excuse me. Yes, you are referring to what we have called Sandworm threat. It attacked the Ukraine two different times over the last year shutting down power. Interestingly, they got back online relatively fast because they went back to manual movements.

Here in the U.S. I think we are probably more advanced on our security of those power grids. More than that, I think that our people are trained to be able to get back online manually because of threats in storms and natural disasters that they have trained to be able to get back online and to be able to do that manually.

That said, there is always going to be susceptibility, and with the latest Ellen Nakashima article that came out yesterday advising of a new more advanced threat, I am sure that our power grid operators and Government are looking at how to protect against those.

Mr. RUSH. I want to thank you, Madam Chair, and I yield back.

Mrs. BLACKBURN. I thank the gentleman. Mrs. Brooks, you are recognized for 5 minutes.

Mrs. BROOKS. Thank you, Madam Chairman, and thank you to all of our panelists for sharing your background and your wisdom with us. It seems that part of the problem we face is that cyber attacks when we talk about cybersecurity it is moving far faster, it seems, than our cyber defenses and the bad guys only have to be right once while the good guys have to be right all of the time.

I am a former U.S. attorney and but from '01 to '07 when we were really standing up cyber teams and I certainly know the FBI and obviously NSA and others have really beefed up their cybersecurity, but yet I am a bit troubled that—because I was just, you know, Googling big cyber cases and so forth and they seem to be happening more in other countries than they are happening in our country.

And I am just curious how much cooperation is there with the private sector lending your advice to the Government sector in prosecuting and enforcing our cyber laws. And I am concerned that your expertise and the expertise of those in your industry, it is hard for Government to bring folks in. As you said, I believe, Mr. Yoran that often it goes the other way. They start in Government and then go out to the private sector.

But yet if we aren't cooperating and I think at a very different level than we currently are, and I appreciate your work and what the commissions have done and recommendations and so forth, but I think we need to accelerate it in a much greater way of how we can prevent, not just prevent because you are all focused on preventing, but if we don't actually prosecute. And Mr. Wright, would you like to start us out?

Mr. WRIGHT. Sure.

Mrs. BROOKS. And I really need to hear what your thoughts are about the level of Government's willingness to bring your expertise to the table to help us, you know, stop these people by actually prosecuting.

Mr. WRIGHT. Yes, I think you are making an absolute, excellent point there. There is a focus on protection, whereas rarely do we speak about deterrents. One of the main deterrents is prosecuting. I would say that the FBI in particular has gotten much better. In fact, I would put them at very good at this point. They are recruiting the right people. They are going after the cybercriminals. And maybe if you don't read about it as much here in the United States it is because a lot of our adversaries, cybercrime adversaries, are sitting overseas; very tough to prosecute in those cases.

But I will tell you one good story that happened right at the beginning of this year. Symantec partnered with the FBI and worked on a case we referred to as Bayrob. It went on for 9 years. We had finally culminated in the arrest and extradition of three Romanian citizens that are currently sitting here in the U.S. awaiting trial.

Those connections that private-sector companies are making with law enforcement are getting better every day. They are getting more and more trusted. I actually think that is a good news story for us now. But I think focusing on some sort of deterrents is really important because today cybercrime has all upside and no downside. There are no risks, very few risks involved in being in cybercrime.

Mrs. BROOKS. Thank you. Mr. Yoran, any comments you might have and should we be looking at a different model of how Government is working with the private sector to bring people to justice? Because 9 years and three defendants doesn't sound like enough to me, but I applaud it—but 9 years and three defendants.

Mr. YORAN. And I am sure there is a lot of detail to that case and will point to many follow-on cases and other investigations. I think you bring up a very important point. There are many cooperative efforts between law enforcement and private industry.

A few areas where private industry has really augmented what has been traditional Government function is in the area of attack attribution and threat intelligence of which Symantec, you know, is a very active participant. And that can aid and assist law enforcement and also help create deterrents whether it is through naming and shaming or other means.

There also remains, I think, a reasonable gap between the interest of law enforcement and those trying to defend networks where there are instances where, you know, law enforcement officials would like to, for the purposes of prosecuting a crime, leave systems open and to continue to monitor how a crime is unfolding, whereas those trying to defend networks frequently care a little bit less about who is doing it and more about cleaning up their systems.

Mrs. BROOKS. My time is up, but if any of you would have any other comments you would like to make, I would certainly appreciate any written comments on it. Thank you. I yield back.

Mrs. BLACKBURN. Thank you, gentlelady, and Mr. Costello for 5 minutes.

Mr. COSTELLO. Thank you. Mr. Wright, from your experience working on both the Federal side and industry sides of cybersecurity, I want to ask you this question. And this comes from a conversation I had with somebody pretty high up the food chain on this issue. Mobile device hardware, how serious of a problem is it that DOD and the U.S. Government rely on foreign IT hardware as well as just the consumer products that we utilize in that space? Many of it is foreign manufactured or foreign designed and specifically I have heard that there are times when the capacity or capability of a particular device far exceeds, the potential for it far exceeds what the realization of that device is actually for. Does that make sense?

Mr. WRIGHT. So I think the capacity and capability——

Mr. COSTELLO. In other words you can have more with——

Mr. WRIGHT. Far exceeds, I am sorry? What——

Mr. COSTELLO. Far exceeds what a consumer is actually intending to utilize it for.

Mr. WRIGHT. Well, I think that certainly on this side, mobile phone consumers are sort of just hitting the beginning of what they eventually are going to do with mobile devices. As far as concern about where those mobile devices are being built, you know, I think that some of these supply chains are always going to be important and can open up some possible vulnerabilities.

So we need to be able to have an understanding of where not only the device is put together but where those individual pieces are manufactured and pulled into the device, because they can certainly open yourself up to vulnerabilities.

Mr. COSTELLO. I want to pick up on the line of inquiry that Mrs. Brooks was pursuing and that is, it seems to me distinguishing between lawful legitimate activity and unlawful activity, someone engaged in a cybersecurity crime is often difficult to discern until it is too late. And whether it is the cloud, whether it is wireless access points, I was reading a little bit in the testimony about the mobile device management solutions.

The question I have here is, is our criminal code, does it reflect the technological capacity of cybercrime as it stands today or are we sort of, is it antiquated? Does it need to evolve or does it need to be, does it need to reflect the way that criminal activity occurs, because often times a crime could be happening and yet we are not able to call it a crime because the actual malware or the actual money hasn't been stolen or the last piece of the crime which would actually make it criminal hasn't yet occurred. Does that make sense?

And so my question to any of you is, be it with wireless access points, be it with just how often we use the cloud, do you see certain types of cybercriminal activity where our criminal code does not properly reflect what is happening day in and day out in such a manner that we are able to go and prevent crimes from happening because our criminal code does not have the elements to be able to have us sufficiently charge them with a crime early enough before it is too late, anyone?

Ms. TODT. I think the industry, obviously industry has a thoughtful perspective on this and I know Symantec has done some tremendous work in this space. There is an entity called the National Cyber-Forensics & Training Alliance center which works with the FBI with consumers with law enforcement to understand where the criminal code is aligned with cybercrime.

And I know that they are working on revising it where necessary, because I think, you know, to the point that was made, rightly, it is this deterrents effort. But updating just as we need to do across all elements of cybersecurity we tend to have a physical approach to cybercrime sometimes and understanding that the NCFTA, I believe, is looking at that specifically.

Mr. COSTELLO. Yes.

Mr. WRIGHT. I would just say, yes, I agree there are some sort of unique things about pursuing and prosecuting a cyber case, chain of custody of evidence is one of them.

Mr. COSTELLO. Right.

Mr. WRIGHT. I can't think of sort of specific incidences where we are crosswise with the laws, but that is certainly something I think they could look into. There is one area, the way that we share information, prosecutorial information with other countries, our MLAT process, our Mutual Legal Assistance Treaties, I believe are outdated. They need to be, they probably need to be revised so that we can share information, we could have information shared with us so that we can prosecute better.

Mr. COSTELLO. The concern I have—and my time is over—is, just given the lack or small number of instances where we are able to prosecute on this, tells me that there is just too much, there is no risk. I think that was the term you used. There is no risk to not engage in cybersecurity crimes when you are these actors. And that is terribly concerning, and it just raises the question to me on the criminal side of it: Is there more that we can do to enable the prosecution of this more easily? I yield back.

Mrs. BLACKBURN. The gentleman yields back, and there are no further Members seeking time for questions. Pursuant to committee rules, I remind Members that they have 10 business days to submit additional questions.

And I think you all are probably aware you have got written questions coming to you. We would ask that you respond to those written questions within 10 business days, and get that back to us. It is a hearing where there is a good bit of interest, and we look forward to moving forward on this issue this year.

So, seeing no further business to come to the subcommittee today, the committee is adjourned.

[Whereupon, at 12:04 p.m., the subcommittee was adjourned.]

[Material submitted for inclusion in the record follows:]

GREG WALDEN, OREGON
CHAIRMAN

FRANK PALLONE, JR., NEW JERSEY
RANKING MEMBER

ONE HUNDRED FIFTEENTH CONGRESS

Congress of the United States

House of Representatives

COMMITTEE ON ENERGY AND COMMERCE
2125 RAYBURN HOUSE OFFICE BUILDING
WASHINGTON, DC 20515–6115

Majority (202) 225–2927
Minority (202) 225–3641

September 13, 2017

Mr. Bill Wright
Director, Government Affairs and Senior Policy Counsel
Symantec
700 13th Street, N.W.; Suite 1150
Washington, DC 20005

Dear Mr. Wright:

Thank you for appearing before the Subcommittee on Communications and Technology on Tuesday, June 13, 2017, to testify at the hearing entitled "Promoting Security in Wireless Technology."

Pursuant to the Rules of the Committee on Energy and Commerce, the hearing record remains open for ten business days to permit Members to submit additional questions for the record, which are attached. The format of your responses to these questions should be as follows: (1) the name of the Member whose question you are addressing, (2) the complete text of the question you are addressing in bold, and (3) your answer to that question in plain text.

To facilitate the printing of the hearing record, please respond to these questions by the close of business on Wednesday September 27, 2017. Your responses should be mailed to Evan M. Viau, Legislative Clerk, Committee on Energy and Commerce, 2125 Rayburn House Office Building, Washington, DC 20515 and e-mailed in Word format to Evan.Viau@mail.house.gov

Thank you again for your time and effort preparing and delivering testimony before the Subcommittee.

Sincerely,

Marsha Blackburn
Chairman
Subcommittee on Communications and Technology

cc: The Honorable Mike Doyle, Ranking Member, Subcommittee on Communication and Technology

Attachment

Post-Hearing Questions for the Record

Submitted to Bill Wright

"Promoting Security in Wireless Technology"

June 13, 2017

The Honorable Anna G. Eshoo

1. Please provide your single topline cybersecurity recommendation to the Subcommittee?

As cyber attacks become increasingly more sophisticated, the natural reaction is to counter with equally more sophisticated defenses. It makes sense, but even the most sophisticated defense won't be very effective if you haven't covered the fundamentals of cybersecurity first. The role of good cyber hygiene can't be overstated. The Online Trust Alliance (OTA) conducted a study and analysis of 500 breaches in 2015 and determined that 90% of them could have been prevented with good cyber hygiene practices – these include good password management policies, Patching and software updates, Least Privilege User Access, Strong security software, back-up strategy, regular pen testing, mobile device management program. With these basic cyber hygiene steps, the vast percentage of successful cyber attacks can be prevented.

The Honorable Eliot Engel

1. In response to recent investigative reporting from Pro-Publica and Gizmodo, I sent a letter with the Ranking Member Mike Doyle and about two dozen of our colleagues to White House Counsel Don McGahn regarding cybersecurity vulnerabilities at the President's properties, including and especially his retreat at Mar-a-Lago. I'd like to discuss some of those vulnerabilities. For starters, it appears that several wireless networks at Mar-a-Lago are encrypted with the WEP standard.

    a. Can you discuss the security of the WEP standard? Is it secure?

Most wireless access points have the ability to enable one of three wireless encryption standards: Wired Equivalent Privacy (WEP), Wi-Fi Protected Access (WPA) or WPA2. WEP was developed in the late 1990's as the first encryption algorithm for the 802.11 standard and was designed to prevent hackers from snooping on wireless data as it is transmitted between clients and access points. Several critical flaws have been identified in WEP since 2001. In addition to these vulnerabilities, the weak encryption incorporated into WEP makes it less secure than WPA or WPA2.

    b. If the wireless networks at Mar-a-Lago are encrypted with the WEP standard, what sorts of information could a foreign governments or cybercriminals have access to?

I do not have any specific insight or knowledge into the level of security of the wireless network or the kinds of information that resides at Mar-a-Lago.

     c.   If someone was successful in compromising those wireless networks, could a foreign government turn on the microphone or cameras for devices connected to that network to collect intelligence.

I do not have any specific insight or knowledge into the level of security of the wireless network at Mar-a-Lago. Once a network is compromised, much would depend on the security of individual devices.

     2.   Unsecured wireless printers were also found at Mar-a-Lago.

     a.   Could you explain how something as simple as an unsecured wireless printer can affect the larger wireless network at a facility like Mar-a-Lago?

An unsecured wireless printer could be a targeted device for attackers to enter an organization. While IT security is focused on protect is focused on protecting computers, a vulnerable and accessible wireless printer could provide the access point to an organization. From there, it is possible for an attacker to move through the network.

     b.   Could a vulnerability like this lead to the unauthorized dissemination of sensitive information?

It is possible for an attacker to intercept documents being sent to a printer over the wireless network. However, without knowing any particulars of the security in place, I am unwilling to speculate what information could be disseminated.

     c.   How difficult would it be to secure an unsecured printer and fix this problem altogether?

Some vulnerabilities are specific to the make and model of the printer. But by following best practice the printer can be made secure.

- *Make sure the printer is up to date with patches to remove known vulnerabilities*
- *Make sure all default passwords have been changed*
- *Make sure that WPA2 encryption is being used*
- *Make sure printer is behind the organization's firewall*
- *Close all network ports on the printer that are not being used*

Depending on the use and location of the printer limiting who can print to the printer and who has physical access to it is a good idea.

<table>
<tr><td>GREG WALDEN, OREGON
CHAIRMAN</td><td>FRANK PALLONE, JR., NEW JERSEY
RANKING MEMBER</td></tr>
</table>

ONE HUNDRED FIFTEENTH CONGRESS

Congress of the United States

House of Representatives

COMMITTEE ON ENERGY AND COMMERCE

2125 RAYBURN HOUSE OFFICE BUILDING

WASHINGTON, DC 20515–6115

Majority (202) 225-2927
Minority (202) 225-3641

September 13, 2017

Mr. Amit Yoran
Chairman and CEO
Tenable Network Security
7021 Columbia Gateway Drive; Suite 500
Columbia, MD 21046

Dear Mr. Yoran:

Thank you for appearing before the Subcommittee on Communications and Technology on Tuesday, June 13, 2017, to testify at the hearing entitled "Promoting Security in Wireless Technology."

Pursuant to the Rules of the Committee on Energy and Commerce, the hearing record remains open for ten business days to permit Members to submit additional questions for the record, which are attached. The format of your responses to these questions should be as follows: (1) the name of the Member whose question you are addressing, (2) the complete text of the question you are addressing in bold, and (3) your answer to that question in plain text.

To facilitate the printing of the hearing record, please respond to these questions by the close of business on Wednesday September 27, 2017. Your responses should be mailed to Evan M. Viau, Legislative Clerk, Committee on Energy and Commerce, 2125 Rayburn House Office Building, Washington, DC 20515 and e-mailed in Word format to Evan.Viau@mail.house.gov

Thank you again for your time and effort preparing and delivering testimony before the Subcommittee.

Sincerely,

Marsha Blackburn
Chairman
Subcommittee on Communications and Technology

cc: The Honorable Mike Doyle, Ranking Member, Subcommittee on Communication and Technology

Attachment

The Honorable Anna G. Eshoo

- **Please provide your single topline cybersecurity recommendation to the Subcommittee**

We recommend a new approach to security awareness that involves fully knowing and understanding the federal government's cyber exposure. Assets have expanded from a laptop or server to a complex mix of digital computer platforms and devices that represent the modern attack surface, where the assets themselves and their associated vulnerabilities are constantly expanding, contracting and evolving. This elastic attack surface has created a massive gap in the government's ability to truly understand their cyber exposure at any given time. The federal government needs live visibility into every asset on any computing environment to manage, measure and reduce cyber risk. This can be achieved by modernizing legacy IT systems.

- **Recent reports and Congressional testimony from former FBI Director James Comey indicate that intrusions into state and local election systems during the 2016 elections were worse than initially thought. Given that there are over 3,000 counties in the United States that use a variety of technologies to manage elections, I'm highly concerned about the vulnerability of these systems.**

  - **What do you recommend to be done to assist counties in protecting against these threats to our democracy?**

We recommend each county implement cyber hygiene best practices and take steps that will enable them to truly understand their cyber exposure at all times. Good cyber hygiene means knowing what is on your network and systems in order to identify risks and vulnerabilities. Without that step, cybersecurity efforts are far less likely to be effective. Knowing your network is more than just the first step in a cybersecurity exercise; it has to be a continuous step. A modern approach to cybersecurity is based not only on scanning, but discovery of unknown assets and assessing their vulnerability. With the right technology, it is possible for organizations to gain real-time visibility into their asset base, where they are exposed, and the insight to help prioritize the risks that matter most.

We support legislation, such as Rep. Anna Eshoo's The Promoting Good Cyber Hygiene Act, that will establish a baseline set of voluntary best practices to achieve good cyber hygiene and will instruct agencies to consider the benefits of cybersecurity measures like data loss prevention and multi-factor authentication. We also believe the bipartisan State Cyber Resiliency Act is a positive step to boost cybersecurity by funding grants for cybersecurity planning and implantation through FEMA. By having this funding focus on states that have found themselves at the center of a cyber attack, our nation can provide tools to protect our citizens and democracy.

Please contact James Hayes, Vice President, Tenable Global Government Affairs at ████████████████ or vis phone at ███████████

Sincerely,

James L. Hayes
Tenable Network Security
Vice President, Government Affairs

GREG WALDEN, OREGON
CHAIRMAN

FRANK PALLONE, JR., NEW JERSEY
RANKING MEMBER

ONE HUNDRED FIFTEENTH CONGRESS

Congress of the United States

House of Representatives

COMMITTEE ON ENERGY AND COMMERCE
2125 RAYBURN HOUSE OFFICE BUILDING
WASHINGTON, DC 20515–6115

Majority (202) 225–2927
Minority (202) 225–3641

September 13, 2017

Dr. Charles Clancy
Director and Professor
Hume Center for National Security and Technology
Virginia Tech
900 North Glebe Road
Arlington, VA 22203

Dear Dr. Clancy:

Thank you for appearing before the Subcommittee on Communications and Technology on Tuesday, June 13, 2017, to testify at the hearing entitled "Promoting Security in Wireless Technology."

Pursuant to the Rules of the Committee on Energy and Commerce, the hearing record remains open for ten business days to permit Members to submit additional questions for the record, which are attached. The format of your responses to these questions should be as follows: (1) the name of the Member whose question you are addressing, (2) the complete text of the question you are addressing in bold, and (3) your answer to that question in plain text.

To facilitate the printing of the hearing record, please respond to these questions by the close of business on Wednesday September 27, 2017. Your responses should be mailed to Evan M. Viau, Legislative Clerk, Committee on Energy and Commerce, 2125 Rayburn House Office Building, Washington, DC 20515 and e-mailed in Word format to Evan.Viau@mail.house.gov.

Thank you again for your time and effort preparing and delivering testimony before the Subcommittee.

Sincerely,

Marsha Blackburn
Chairman
Subcommittee on Communications and Technology

Cc: The Honorable Mike Doyle,, Ranking Member, Subcommittee on Communication and Technology

Attachment

Responses to *Questions for the Record*

Dr. Charles Clancy, Professor of Electrical and Computer Engineering, Virginia Tech

before the House Energy and Commerce Committee, Subcommittee on Communications and Technology, Hearing on Promoting Security in Wireless Technologies

September 27, 2017

The following document provides responses to the questions for the record for the hearing entitled "Promoting Security in Wireless Technology" on June 13, 2017.

The Honorable Anna G. Eshoo – (1) Please provide your single topline cybersecurity recommendation to the Subcommittee.

Cybersecurity is a domain of partnership. Rarely does one organization owns enough of digital ecosystem to unilaterally achieve needed security objectives. Thus the Subcommittee should foster a philosophy of partnership when considering new cybersecurity legislative action. Legislation such the *Cybersecurity Information Sharing Act of 2015* is an excellent example of positive contributions in this space, along with executive actions like Executive Order 13636, *Improving Critical Infrastructure Cybersecurity*, and the resulting NIST Cybersecurity Framework. The proposed Warner-Gardner-Wyden-Daines *Cybersecurity Improvement Act of 2017* is also directionally correct in its approach to tackling new security challenges resulting from the Internet of Things (IoT), specifically its proposed use of industry-led device certification standards.

The Honorable Anna G. Eshoo – (2) Recent reports and Congressional testimony from former FBI Director James Comey indicate that intrusions into state and local election systems during the 2016 elections were worse that initially thought. Given that there are over 3,000 countries in the United States that use a variety of technologies to mange elections, I'm highly concerned about the vulnerability of these systems. (a) What do you recommend be done to assets counties in protecting against these threats to our democracy?

The electronic and information systems that support voting in the United States are a critical component in the integrity of our election process. In 2002 Congress passed the *Help America Vote Act* which required the National Institute for Science and Technology (NIST) to develop the Voluntary Voting System Guidelines (VVSG) which includes cybersecurity specifications for voting infrastructure. As of 2016, 47 states used these guidelines to varying degrees – some states build to the standards while others have their infrastructure fully certified. Of the 21 states informed by the Department of Homeland Security (DHS) that their voting systems were targeted, all levels of VVSG adoption are represented.

It is critical that if these systems are targeted by hackers in future elections that they are able to detect and prevent such attacks from being successful. One way to accomplish this is to incentivize states and counties to have fully-certified voting systems under the VVSG, and to implement a broader cybersecurity risk management strategy under the NIST Cybersecurity Framework. Realistically accomplishing such certifications will require federal subsidy of associated costs, perhaps through a block grant program to states to support these improvements.

GREG WALDEN, OREGON
CHAIRMAN

FRANK PALLONE, JR., NEW JERSEY
RANKING MEMBER

ONE HUNDRED FIFTEENTH CONGRESS

Congress of the United States

House of Representatives

COMMITTEE ON ENERGY AND COMMERCE
2125 RAYBURN HOUSE OFFICE BUILDING
WASHINGTON, DC 20515–6115

Majority (202) 225–2927
Minority (202) 225–3641

September 13, 2017

Ms. Kiersten Todt
Managing Partner
Liberty Group Ventures
3033 Wilson Boulevard; Suite 700
Arlington, VA 22201

Dear Ms. Todt:

Thank you for appearing before the Subcommittee on Communications and Technology on Tuesday, June 13, 2017, to testify at the hearing entitled "Promoting Security in Wireless Technology."

Pursuant to the Rules of the Committee on Energy and Commerce, the hearing record remains open for ten business days to permit Members to submit additional questions for the record, which are attached. The format of your responses to these questions should be as follows: (1) the name of the Member whose question you are addressing, (2) the complete text of the question you are addressing in bold, and (3) your answer to that question in plain text.

To facilitate the printing of the hearing record, please respond to these questions by the close of business on Wednesday September 27, 2017. Your responses should be mailed to Evan M. Viau, Legislative Clerk, Committee on Energy and Commerce, 2125 Rayburn House Office Building, Washington, DC 20515 and e-mailed in Word format to Evan.Viau@mail.house.gov

Thank you again for your time and effort preparing and delivering testimony before the Subcommittee.

Sincerely,

Marsha Blackburn
Chairman
Subcommittee on Communications and Technology

cc: The Honorable Mike Doyle, Ranking Member, Subcommittee on Communication and Technology

Attachment

Questions for the Record

Submitted by Kiersten E. Todt, President and Managing Partner, Liberty Group Ventures, LLC

The Honorable Frank Pallone, Jr.

Could the FCC have known so quickly that it experienced a cyber attack? How could the Commission be sure it was not merely experiencing a high volume of people attempting to comment on its proposal following the segment?

It would have been very difficult for the FCC to have known so quickly. If the FCC had the infrastructure required to be able to diagnose the issue so immediately, it likely would not have experienced the issue in the first place.

The Honorable Anna G. Eshoo
Please provide your single topline cybersecurity recommendation to the Subcommittee.

The White House needs to have an individual solely responsible for cybersecurity, reporting directly to the President. The current structure sets us up for failure if events across multiple responsibilities in the portfolio of the current Assistant to the President responsible for cybersecurity (in addition to domestic terrorism, homeland security, including natural disasters) happen simultaneously.

The Honorable Eliot Engel

Questions #1 and #2

I don't have a deep technical background on the WEP standard.

I will, however, offer perspectives on potential vulnerabilities at Mar-a-Lago. Given the interdependencies of the Mar-a-Lago infrastructure, similar to many residential infrastructures, any vulnerable access point that is violated will open up access to the broader network, if appropriate security measures have not been taken. This access violation has the potential to lead to unauthorized access to the network and the data that resides on the network.

Question #3
Do you support more information sharing across government, and do you think this approach of using such information to start additional investigations and reports would be helpful?

Yes, I support increased information sharing across government. The government needs to lead by example and demonstrate the efficiencies that evolve from understanding and examining threats, incidents, and responses across all agencies.